Budgies
in Your Life

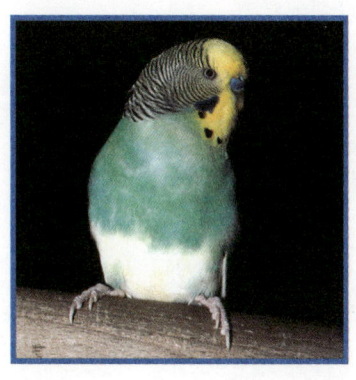

Critter Press

Critter Press
A Simon & Schuster Macmillan Company
1633 Broadway
New York, NY 10019

Copyright © 1997 by **Critter Press**

Budgies in Your Life is an abridged edition of *The Budgie: An Owner's Guide to a Happy Healthy Pet* first published in 1997.

All rights reserved. No part of this book may be reprodcued or transmitted in any for or by means, electronic or mechanical, including photocopying, recording, or by any information storage and retrieval system, without permission in writing from the Publisher.

MACMILLAN is a registered trademark of Macmillan, Inc.

ISBN: 0-87605-434-3

Cataloging-in-Publication Data is available upon request from the Library of Congress.

Manufactured in the United States of America

10 9 8 7 6 5 4 3 2 1

SERIES DIRECTOR: AMANDA PISANI
ASSISTANT SERIES DIRECTOR: JENNIFER LIBERTS
ILLUSTRATION BY CASEY PRICE
BOOK DESIGN BY MICHELE LASEAU
COVER DESIGN BY AMY TROMBAT
PRODUCTION BY JOHN CARROLL, KATHLEEN CAULFIELD, TRUDY COLER, STEPHANIE HAMMETT, CLINT LAHNEN, DENNIS SHEEHAN, TERRI SHEEHAN

Photography: cover photos by *B. Everett Webb*
Joan Balzarini: title page
B. Everett Webb: 2–3, 5, 10, 13, 15, 17, 18, 20–21, 22, 25, 30, 44, 48, 73, 81, 83, 91
Reneé Stockdale: 6, 8, 9, 19, 23, 24, 27, 28, 33, 34, 35, 37, 39, 40, 41, 42, 43, 46, 49, 50, 51, 53, 54, 59, 66, 69, 78, 80, 84, 85, 86, 89,
Scott Kiernan / Zuma Press: 29

Contents

part one
Welcome to the World of the Budgie
chapter **1** Choosing a Budgie *5*

part two
Living with a Budgie
chapter **2** Better Budgie Care *22*
chapter **3** Bringing Your Budgie Home *29*
chapter **4** Feeding Your Budgie *41*
chapter **5** Grooming Your Budgie *48*
chapter **6** Your Budgie's Physical Health *54*

part three
Enjoying Your Budgie
chapter **7** Budgie Behavior *78*

part four
Beyond the Basics
chapter **8** For More Information *92*

part one
Welcome to the World of the

Budgie

External Features of the Budgerigar

chapter

1

Choosing a
Budgie

Let's look at the background of your chosen bird, the budgerigar. Some of you may know budgerigars by their common nickname, budgies. Others may call them parakeets. Both are correct, since the term parakeet generally describes any long-tailed parrot.

True Australians

Budgies come from Australia, where they live in large communal flocks. (These large flocks make budgies naturally sociable birds. If you keep a single pet bird, make sure you fulfill its need for companionship by spending time with it each day.) Many wild budgerigars are found in central Australia, which is a harsh, arid land. To cope with these extreme conditions, budgies have adapted to surviving on minimal food and water requirements.

Budgies that live in central Australia have adapted to the harshness of the environment by reproducing at an early age and having many chicks in the hope that some will survive the rigors of life in that part of the country.

1

Welcome to the World of the Budgie

Budgies that live on the coast and in the central southern areas, where the climate is less extreme, do not demonstrate this ability to breed early and often.

The budgie's name is said to come from an Aboriginal phrase that means "good to eat," although I can't imagine eating such personable little birds. The species' scientific name, *Melopsittacus undulatus*, literally means "song parrot with wavy lines," which refers to the birds' melodic voices and the wavy bars across their backs and wings. These wavy lines help wild budgies camouflage themselves in the Australian grasslands so they are less obvious to predators. In the past, budgies were also called shell parrots, warbling grass parakeets and zebra parrots.

The wavy lines on the budgie's back and wings help to camouflage it in the wild.

So Why Is the Budgie So Popular?

Some of the reasons bird lovers are attracted to budgerigars include their manageable size, their gentleness, their nondestructiveness, the ease with which they can be handled and tamed, their sociable nature and their talking ability, although the last shouldn't be the sole reason for choosing a budgie or any other pet bird.

A budgie's size makes it an easily handled pet for bird lovers, young or old. A healthy budgie measures about 7 inches from the top of its head to the tip of its tail, and it weighs about 30 grams (1.05 ounces). This small bird comes with a quiet, pleasant voice and a manageable beak. Since noise and the potential for painful bites deter some potential bird owners, the budgie offers a welcome alternative from ear-splitting shrieks or serious wounds from bites.

Because budgies have been kept as pets for so many years, some people consider them one of the few domesticated pet birds. They seem to enjoy people and being part of an active family. They also seem to want to please their owners by learning tricks or learning to talk, although I can't guarantee that your budgie will be a trickster or a talker. Please choose a budgie as a pet because you want to share your home with a bird and appreciate it for the unique being that it is, not because you're looking for a feathered mimic.

Before you decide to bring a budgie into your life, you'll need to consider a few questions first. Do you have time to care for one properly? Can you have pets where you live? Can you live with a little mess (seed hulls, feathers and discarded food) in your home? Can you tolerate, and appreciate, a little noise (the amount made by one exuberant budgie) as part of your daily routine?

Why a Bird?

If you've answered "yes" to all these, you're a good candidate for bird ownership. Now your next question might be "Why do I want a bird?" Here are some of the answers you might come up with:

Birds are relatively quiet pets. Unless you have a particularly vocal macaw or cockatoo, most birds aren't likely to annoy the neighbors the way a barking dog or a yowling cat can. In many rental situations, birds aren't even considered pets, which means you can keep them without having to surrender a sizable security deposit to your landlord.

If you do rent an apartment or house and you do own a bird, please be responsible enough to keep your pet from defecating on carpets, peeling wallpaper or damaging paint. If your bird damages something in the apartment or house, please offer to have the damage repaired. Future pet owners who follow in your footsteps will thank you because you've set a responsible example and made it easier for them to show the landlord that pet owners care enough about their pets and their rental situation to take care of any problems caused by the animals.

1

Welcome to the World of the Budgie

Amusing and friendly interaction is one of the many reasons people choose a budgie for a pet.

Birds' small size makes them good pets for today's smaller living spaces. More of us are living in apartments, mobile or manufactured homes and condominiums, which makes the ownership of large pets that need yards and lots of regular exercise awkward and inconvenient. Birds just seem to fit better in apartments, condos, mobile homes and other smaller living spaces.

Birds may be easier to maintain than dogs and cats. As one who has had all three types of pets, I think the daily maintenance time a bird requires may be less than a dog or cat. Birds don't have to be walked; they don't require as much grooming as a longhaired dog or cat nor do they shed as much. And there's only a cage and small bowls to clean up, instead of bowls and a litter box for a cat or the whole yard in the case of a dog.

Birds interact well with their owners. Although a bird isn't as blindly loyal as the average dog, it isn't as aloof as many cats I've known, either. As an added bonus, many birds can learn to whistle or talk, which is beyond the range of canine and feline ability and which many owners find amusing or entertaining.

Birds are long-lived pets. A cockatoo named King Tut greeted visitors at the San Diego Zoo for 70 years, and *Bird Talk* magazine reported on a documented 106-year-old Amazon in Alaska. Many bird owners I know have made provisions for their larger parrots in their wills. Smaller birds can live long lives, too; the *Guinness Book of Records* reports an almost 30-year-old budgerigar in Great Britain.

Birds require consistent, but not constant, attention. This can be a plus for today's busy single people and families. While birds can't be ignored completely, they are content to entertain themselves for part of the day while their owners are busy elsewhere.

I can't tell you how many of my evenings have been brightened with the presence of my bird, Sindbad. He is content to sit on my lap and have his back rubbed or his head scratched while we watch TV together. He asks for very little except regular feedings and cage cleanings and a bit of attention each day, and he offers companionship and unconditional love in return.

Finally, **birds are intelligent pets.** Whoever coined the phrase "birdbrain" didn't truly appreciate how smart some birds are. Some larger parrots have scored at levels comparable to chimpanzees, dolphins and preschool age children on intelligence tests.

Are you purchasing a parakeet on a whim because you're attracted to its bright colors? Are you rescuing a bird from its aggressive cagemates? Are you buying a bird you otherwise feel sorry for? Noble though some of these reasons are, none of them is a good reason for purchasing a pet bird. Birds purchased for their pretty colors may soon be ignored or neglected by owners whose attentions have been captured by another fancy, and small, timid birds may be hiding signs of illness that can be difficult and costly to cure and that can cause an owner much heartache in the process.

If you feel the urge to become a bird owner, and you've bought this book instead, you're on the right road. If you

Budgies may be good pets for people who have limited space to house a pet.

1
Welcome to the World of the Budgie

purchased this book along with your parakeet, this is also a good first step, or if you've picked up this book after having your bird a few weeks or months, congratulations! You're on the road to responsible bird ownership.

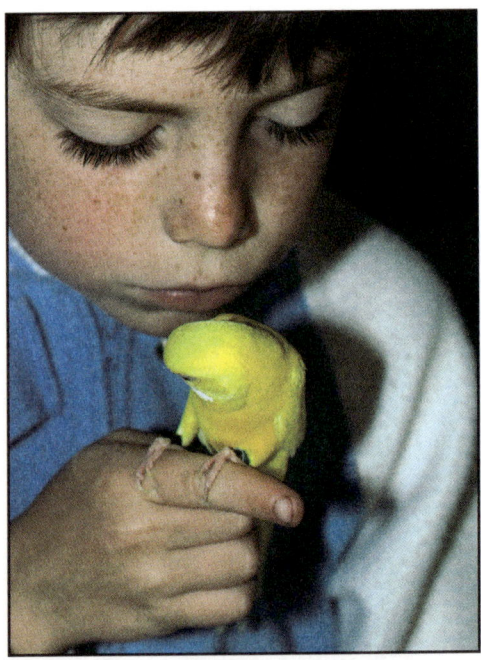

Children who know how to properly handle birds can be great friends with a pet budgie.

Budgies and Children

If you plan to purchase a budgie as a child's pet, please keep the following in mind. Children in the primary grades may need some help from their parents or from older siblings in caring for their new pet. Children in the intermediate grades should be ready for the responsibility of bird ownership with limited parental supervision. Or the bird can just be "a family pet" with each family member being responsible for some aspect of the bird's care. Even the youngest family members can help out by selecting healthful foods for the bird on a trip to the market or picking out a safe, colorful toy at the bird store.

Parents need to remind their children of the following when they're around birds:

1. Approach the cage quietly. Birds don't like to be surprised.
2. Talk softly to the bird. Don't scream or yell at it.
3. Don't shake or hit the cage.
4. Don't poke at the bird or its cage with your fingers, sticks, pencils or other items.
5. If you're allowed to take the bird out of its cage, handle it gently.

6. Don't take the bird outside. In unfamiliar surroundings (such as the outdoors), birds can become confused and fly away from their owners. Most are never recovered.

7. Respect the bird's need for quiet time.

I'd like to remind adults to please not give any live pet as a holiday present. Birthdays, Christmas, Hanukkah and other holidays are exciting but stressful times for both people and animals. A pet coming to a new home is under enough stress just by joining its new family; don't add to its stress by bringing it home for a holiday. Instead, give the child pet-care accessories for the actual celebration and a gift certificate that will allow the child to select his or her pet (with proper parental permission, of course) after the excitement of the special day has died down.

> **Parrot Traits**
>
> The budgie is a species of parrot, just like Macaws or Amazons. The traits that all parrot species have in common are
>
> - four toes—two pointing backward and two pointing forward
> - upper beak overhanging the lower
> - broad head and short neck
>
> However, a healthy budgie measures about 7 inches from tip of the head to tip of the tail, while a full-grown Scarlet Macaw can easily reach 40 inches in length.

The Bottom Line

Some things you'll want to think about as you become a budgie owner are:

- the cost of the bird itself
- the cost of its cage and accessories
- the cost of bird food (seeds, formulated diets and fresh foods)
- the cost of toys
- the cost of veterinary care
- how busy your life is already
- who will care for the bird if you go on vacation or are called out of town unexpectedly
- how many other pets you already own
- the size of your home

1

Welcome to the World of the Budgie

If, after considering all these factors, you're still interested in adding a budgie to your home because you want a cheerful companion bird, please read on to learn more about bringing a budgie into your life.

Where Will You Get Your Budgie?

Budgies can be purchased through several sources, including classified newspaper advertisements, bird shows and marts and pet stores. Let's look at each in a bit more detail.

Classified Advertisements

Classified ads are usually placed by private parties who want to place pets in new homes. If the advertiser offers young birds, it is likely to be a private breeder who wants to place a few birds in good homes.

Most pet budgies can leave the breeder's home at around six weeks of age, and the time between six weeks and three months of age is considered by some to be the optimal time to teach a pet budgie to talk and to do tricks. You can tell baby budgies by the series of stripes that cover their heads and necks (the stripes remain on the backs of the birds' necks following the first molt). Young birds also have small, slightly elongated spots on their face masks, while adults have large, round spots, and youngsters also have large, dark eyes that give them particularly endearing looks, where adult birds have well-developed white irises. Baby budgies may also have dark or slightly black beaks.

Some breeders may also offer older birds for sale from time to time. These are most likely breeder birds that are too old to produce chicks but that are still good candidates for pet situations.

If you buy your bird from a private breeder, you will probably be shown only the birds that the breeder has for sale. Do not be offended or upset if you cannot see all the birds that the breeder keeps; some birds are more sensitive than others about the presence of strangers during breeding season, and the sensitive ones may destroy eggs or kill chicks when they're upset. Budgies are less prone to this sensitivity than larger parrots, but a breeder may keep all of his or her nesting pairs in the same area. If, however, a breeder is willing to show you around his or her facility, consider it a special treat and an honor that few people ever have bestowed on them.

Bird Shows and Marts

These offer bird breeders and bird buyers an opportunity to get together to share a love for birds. Bird shows can provide prospective bird owners with the chance to see many different types of birds all in one place (usually far more than many pet shops would keep at a time), which can help you narrow your choices if you're undecided about which species to keep. At a bird show, you can watch to see which birds win consistently, then talk to the breeder of these birds after the show to see if he or she expects any chicks. (This is especially important if you decide to get into showing budgies, because you want to start with winning stock.)

The price of the bird itself is not the only cost of becoming a budgie owner; don't forget about the cost of necessary equipment and veterinary attention when deciding to get a budgie.

A bird mart is a little different than a bird show. At a bird mart, various species of birds and a wide variety of bird-keeping supplies are offered for sale, so you can go and shop to your heart's content.

Pet Stores

Pet stores may or may not be the ideal place to purchase a budgie. You'll have to check with stores in your area to determine if they even sell pets, since many stores chose not to carry livestock beginning in the early 1990s. These will be listed as "pet supply stores" in your phone book and may be the place you'll want to go to get the cage, food, dishes,

1

Welcome to the World of the Budgie

perches, toys and other accessories you'll need once your budgie comes home.

If a store in your area sells live pets, you'll need to visit the store and make sure it's clean and well kept. Walk around the store a bit. Are the floors clean? Do the cages look and smell like they're cleaned regularly? Do the animals in the cages appear alert, well-fed and healthy? Do the cages appear crowded or do the animals inside have some room to move around?

After you've determined whether the store is clean and the employees are pleasant, find out if the staff tries to keep their birds healthy. Do they ask you to wash your hands with a mild disinfectant before handling their birds or between birds? If they do, don't balk at the request. This is for the health of the birds, and it indicates that the store is concerned about keeping its livestock healthy. Buying a healthy bird is much easier and more enjoyable than purchasing a pet with health problems, so don't be afraid to follow the rules in a caring store!

If something about the store, staff or livestock doesn't feel quite right, choose another establishment to do business with. If the store and its livestock meet with your approval (as they often will), then it's time to get down to the all-important task of selecting your budgie.

> ### Budgie Owner's Shopping List
>
> When you go to the pet supply store to pick out your bird's accessories, take a copy of this list along so you won't forget any of the important items your new pet will need to feel right at home!
>
> - a cage
> - open food and water bowls (at least two sets of each for easier dish changing and cage cleaning)
> - perches of varying diameters and materials
> - a sturdy scrub brush to clean the perches
> - food (a good-quality fresh seed mixture or a formulated diet, such as pellets or crumbles)
> - a millet spray (most budgies love this treat!)
> - a powdered vitamin and mineral supplement to sprinkle on your pet's fresh foods
> - a variety of safe, fun toys
> - a cage cover (an old sheet or towel that is free of holes and ravels will serve this purpose nicely)
> - a playgym to allow your budgie time out of its cage and a place to exercise

Choosing the Right Budgie

Look at the budgies that are available for sale. If possible, sit down and watch them for a while. Don't rush this important step. Do some of them seem bolder than the others? Consider those first, because you want a curious, active, robust pet, rather than a shy animal that hides in a corner. Are other budgies sitting off by themselves, seeming to sleep while their cagemates play? Reject any birds that seem too quiet or too sleepy because these signs can indicate illness.

1

Choosing a Budgie

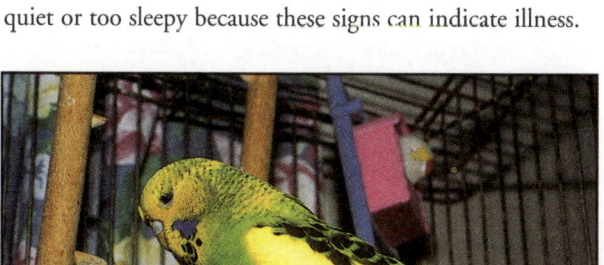

When selecting a budgie, choose a healthy, robust bird rather than the shy animal that hides in the corner.

Remember that healthy birds spend their time doing four main activities—eating, playing, defecating and sleeping—in about equal amounts of time. If you notice that a bird seems to only want to sleep, for instance, reject that bird in favor of another whose routine seems more balanced.

You may think that saving a small, picked-upon budgie from its cagemates seems like the right thing to do, but please resist this urge. You want a strong, healthy, spirited bird, rather than "the runt of the litter." Although it sounds hardhearted, automatically reject any birds that are being bullied, are timid, or that hide in a corner or shy away from you. It will save you some heartache in the end.

If possible, let your budgie choose you. Many pet stores display their budgies in colony situations on playgyms, or a breeder may bring out a clutch of babies for you to look at. If one bird waddles right up to you and wants to play, or if one comes over to check you out and just seems to want to come home with you, that's the bird you want!

1

Welcome to the World of the Budgie

Male or Female?

As you're selecting your budgie, many questions are probably coming to mind, including the sex of your potential pet and if it needs a companion bird.

You may be asking, "Should I get a male or a female budgerigar?" Although males may make slightly better talkers, I'd encourage you to get a young, healthy bird and enjoy it for its full pet potential. If you have your heart set on an older bird, males generally have blue ceres, while females' ceres are brownish, but don't try this sexing test on a young bird because cere color develops as a bird matures.

One or Two?

Another question you may have (especially if you have a busy schedule) is "Should I get one bird or two?" Single pet budgies generally make more affectionate pets, because you and your family become the bird's substitute flock. But a pair of budgies can be pretty entertaining as they chase each other around the cage and encourage each other into all sorts of avian mischief.

Bands are used to identify breeders' stock, and are also helpful in preventing the smuggling of birds into the United States.

One small drawback of owning two pet budgies, especially young ones, is that they may have a tendency to chase each other around the cage, playfully tugging on one another's tail feathers. Sometimes these feathers come out, leaving you with two considerably shorter budgies until the next set of tail feathers grows in.

1
Choosing a Budgie

If you have a pair of birds that suddenly become tailless, check the cage bottom for the feathers and watch your birds to see if they do, indeed, chase and pester each other. If so, you have nothing to worry about. If not, please alert your avian veterinarian to the problem and ask for further guidance. Two birds are also less likely to learn to talk because they can chatter to each other in budgie rather than learning the language of their substitute "flock."

There is also the possibility of territorial behavior on the part of the original bird. This territorial behavior can include bullying the newcomer and keeping him or her away from food and water dishes to the point that the new bird cannot eat or drink.

To avoid this problem, house the birds in separate cages until you can supervise their interactions. Let the birds out together on a neutral playgym and watch how they act with each other. If they seem to get along, you can move their cages closer together so they can become accustomed to being close. Some birds will adjust to having other birds share their cages, while others prefer to remain alone in their cages with other birds close by.

If you keep a pair of budgies, they may be more inclined to bond to each other than to you.

By the same token, don't try to put a new budgie into the cage of a bird you already own, and don't house budgies with other small birds, such as finches, canaries, cockatiels or lovebirds. Budgies may tend to bully finches and canaries, keeping them away from food and water bowls, while cockatiels and lovebirds may exhibit the same behavior toward budgies.

To keep peace in your avian family, make sure every bird has its own cage, food and water bowls. Some budgies will get along with other birds during supervised playtime on a playgym, while others do not "work and play well with others" and enjoy being the only pets out on the gym.

What Does That Band Mean?

As you select your pet, you may notice leg bands on the budgies you're looking at. Bird bands serve several purposes. First, they help identify a particular breeder's stock. They can also help establish an age for your bird, since many of them have the year of hatch as part of the band's code. Finally, in an effort to reduce the number of smuggled birds that are kept as pets in the United States, some states require that certain pet birds be banded with closed, traceable bands. Although this requirement doesn't apply to budgies, it is an indication of things to come in aviculture.

Bringing Your Budgie Home

Quarantine

If you have other birds in your home, you will want to quarantine your budgie for at least 30 days to ensure it doesn't have any diseases that your other birds could catch. To do this, you will need to keep your budgie as far away from your other birds as possible, preferably in a separate room. Feed your newly arrived budgie after you feed your other birds, and be sure to wash your hands thoroughly before and after handling or playing with your new pet. Quarantine is usually just a precautionary measure, but you can't be too safe when your pet's health is involved!

Adjustment Time

Although you will probably want to start playing with your new budgie the minute you bring it home from the breeder,

---

Here are some of the indicators of a healthy budgie. Keep them in mind when selecting your pet.

bright eyes

a clean cere (the area above the bird's beak that covers its nares or nostrils)

upright posture

a full-chested appearance

actively moving around the cage

clean legs and vent

smooth feathers

good appetite

bird mart or store, please resist this temptation. Your new pet will need some time to adjust to its new environment, so be patient. Spend the time instead talking quietly to your new pet, and use its name frequently while you're talking. Move slowly around your budgie for the first few days to avoid startling it.

If you are bringing a new budgie into a one-budgie home, keep the birds in separate cages and supervise their interactions until you are sure they have accepted each together.

Your Budgie's Routine

You will be able to tell when your new pet has settled into its routine, because healthy budgies will spend about equal amounts of time during the day eating, playing, sleeping and defecating. By observation, you will soon recognize your budgie's routine and know what is normal. You may also notice that your bird fluffs or shakes its feathers to greet you, or that it chirps a greeting when you uncover its cage in the morning. If your budgie should learn to talk, it may eventually greet you with a cheery "hello" or "good morning" as you uncover its cage.

part two
Living with a

Budgie

chapter

2

Better Budgie
Care

Ten Steps to Better Bird Care

Bird keeping isn't particularly difficult to do. In fact, if you only do ten things for your budgie for as long as you own it, your bird will have a pretty healthy, well-adjusted life.

Provide an adequate cage in a safe, secure location in your home. The cage should be located in a fairly active part of your home so your bird will feel as if it's part of your family and your daily routine.

Next, clean the cage regularly to protect your pet from illness and to make its surroundings more enjoyable for both of you. Would you want to live in a smelly, dirty house? Your bird doesn't like it either.

Third, clip your bird's wings regularly to ensure its safety. Also bird-proof your home and practice bird safety by closing windows and doors securely before you let your bird out of its cage.

Clean your budgie's cage regularly to protect your pet from illness and to keep its environment pleasant.

Fourth, offer your budgie a varied diet that includes seeds or pellets, fresh vegetables and fruits cut into budgie-sized portions and healthy people food, such as raw or cooked pasta, fresh or toasted whole-wheat bread and unsweetened breakfast cereals.

Your budgie should also have access to clean, fresh drinking water at all times.

Next, establish a good working relationship with a qualified avian veterinarian early on in your bird ownership (preferably on your way home from the pet store or breeder). Don't wait for an emergency to locate a veterinarian.

Sixth, take your budgie to the veterinarian for regular checkups, as well as when you notice a change in its routine. Preventive care helps head off serious problems before they develop.

Seventh, set and maintain a routine for your budgie. Make sure it's fed at about the same time each day, playtime out of its cage occurs regularly and that bedtime is well established.

Eighth, provide an interesting environment for your bird. Entertain and challenge your bird's curiosity with a variety of safe toys. Rotate these toys in and out of your bird's cage regularly, and discard any that become soiled, broken or unsafe.

Ninth, leave a radio or television on for your bird when you are away from home, because a too-quiet environment can be stressful for many birds, and stress can cause illness or other problems for your pet.

Finally, pay attention to your budgie on a consistent basis. Don't lavish abundant attention on the bird when you first bring it home, then gradually lose interest in it. Set aside a portion of each day to spend with your budgie—you'll both enjoy it and your relationship will benefit from it. Besides, wasn't companionship one of the things you were looking for when you picked your budgie as a pet?

Stimulate your budgie by offering a variety of toys and rotating them in and out of its cage.

Now that doesn't seem too difficult, does it? Just devote a little time each day to your pet bird, and soon the two of you will have formed a lifelong bond of trust and mutual enjoyment.

A Routine for You and Your Budgie

A budgie requires a certain level of care *every day* to ensure its health and well-being. Birds are happiest when they are secure and comfortable in a safe environment. You can help your budgie feel more secure by establishing a daily routine and performing the same rituals at around the same time every day. This way, your budgie knows his needs will be met by the people he considers to be his family. Here are some of the things you'll need to do each day for your pet:

- Observe your pet for any changes in its routine (report any changes to your avian veterinarian immediately).

- Offer fresh food and remove old food. Wash food dish thoroughly with detergent and water. Rinse thoroughly and allow to dry.

- Provide fresh water and remove previous dish. Wash dish as above.

- Change paper in cage tray.

- Let the bird out of its cage for supervised playtime.

Finally, you'll want to cover your bird's cage at about the same time every night to indicate bedtime. When you cover the cage, you'll probably hear your bird rustling around for a bit, perhaps getting a drink of water or a last mouthful of seeds before settling in for the night. Keep in mind that your pet will require eight to ten hours of sleep a day, but you can expect that it will take naps during the day to supplement its nightly snooze.

Let your budgie have quality, out-of-cage time with you daily.

Be Alert for Health Indicators

Although it may seem a bit unpleasant to discuss, your bird's droppings require daily monitoring because they can tell you a lot about its general health. Budgies will produce small, flat droppings that appear white in the center with a dark green edge. These droppings are usually composed of equal amounts of fecal material (the green edge), urine (the clear liquid portion) and urates (the white or cream-colored center). A healthy budgie generally eliminates between twenty-five and fifty times a day, although your bird may go more or less often.

Texture and consistency, along with frequency or lack of droppings, can let you know how your pet is feeling. For instance, if a bird eats a lot of fruits and vegetables, its droppings are generally looser and more watery than a bird that eats primarily seeds. But watery droppings can also indicate illness, such as diabetes or kidney problems, that cause a bird to drink more water than usual.

> **Warm Weather Warning**
>
> On a warm day, you may notice your bird sitting with its wings held away from its body, rolling its tongue and holding its mouth open. This is how a bird cools itself off. Watch your bird carefully on warm days because it can overheat quickly, and it may suffer heatstroke, which requires veterinary care. If you live in a warm climate, ask your avian veterinarian how you can protect your bird from this potentially serious problem.

Color can also give an indication of health. Birds that have psittacosis typically have bright, lime-green droppings, while healthy birds have avocado or darker green and white droppings. Birds with liver problems may produce droppings that are yellowish or reddish, while birds that have internal bleeding will produce dark, tarry droppings.

But a color change doesn't necessarily indicate poor health. For instance, birds that eat pelleted diets tend to have darker droppings than their seed-eating companions, while parrots that have splurged on a certain fresh food soon have droppings with that characteristic color. Birds that overindulge on beets, for instance, produce bright red droppings that can look for all the world as though the bird has suffered some serious internal injury. Birds that overdo sweet potatoes, blueberries or raspberries produce orange, blue or red droppings. During pomegranate season, birds that enjoy this fruit develop violet droppings that can look alarming to an unprepared owner.

As part of your daily cage cleaning and observation of your feathered friend, look at its droppings carefully. Learn what is normal for your bird in terms of color, consistency and frequency, and report any changes to your avian veterinarian promptly.

chapter 3

Bringing Your Budgie
Home

Before you bring your feathered friend home, determine where it will live in your house or apartment. Selecting your budgie's cage will be one of the most important decisions you will make for your pet, and where that cage will be located in your home is equally important. Don't wait until you bring your bird home to think this through. You'll want your new pet to settle in to its surroundings right away, rather than adding to its stress by relocating it several times before selecting the right spot for the cage.

Choosing a Cage

Although we didn't do too many things right for my childhood budgie, Charlie, we did select a good home for him. Charlie's cage was large, it had both horizontal and vertical bars for his climbing enjoyment, its food and

3
Living with a Budgie

water dishes slid in and out through holes in the side of the cage (which meant they were easy to get to and made his cage simple to service), it had three or four perches placed at different heights in the cage, and it had a bedsheet for a cover at night.

Some of the cages you'll look at while making your selection are designed to sit on tabletops, while others have built-in or attached stands. Consider which will work best in your home. If yours is an active house with other pets and children in it, a tabletop cage may be better than a cage with a stand that could be knocked over. If you live alone in a small apartment, a cage and stand might be in order. If you do choose a cage with a stand, be sure the stand is steady and fits well with the cage.

Make sure the bars of your bird's cage are close enough together that your budgie will not get his head stuck between them.

Size is Important

When choosing your budgie's cage, remember that it must be large enough to house your bird, its food and water bowls, perches and toys. *Bird Talk* columnist Susan Chamberlain recommends that budgie owners "test cages for 60," which means that the measurements of the cage's length, width and height should total at least 60 when added together. A common size for budgie cages is 18 inches wide, 18 inches high and 24 inches long, which adds up to 60. This would be about the smallest cage to consider if you own a single pet bird. If you have more than one bird or if your bird is an upwardly mobile creature with lots of belongings (toys, food dishes, a bathtub perhaps), a larger cage is in order.

Simply put, buy the largest cage you can afford, because you don't want your pet to feel cramped. Remember, too, that budgies are like little airplanes, flying across an area, rather than little helicopters that hover up and down. For this reason, long rectangular cages that offer horizontal space for short flights are preferred to high, narrow cages that don't provide much flying room.

Acrylic or Wire?

Birdcages are traditionally made of wire, but you may see acrylic cages in magazine advertisements or at your local pet store. These cages are better at containing seed hulls, loose feathers and other debris your bird creates, which may make bird-keeping easier and more enjoyable for you. This is a plus if you want to keep your home clean of birdie debris while still enjoying your pet birds.

I bird-sit a canary that lives in an acrylic cage. It is the easiest bird I have ever cleaned up after, because the feathers, seed hulls and treat scraps remain contained within the cage. All I have to do for this bird is change the cage paper daily and service its food and water bowls twice a day. My own bird's wire cage, on the other hand, requires frequent vacuumings and diligent care.

Although it sounds like a sales pitch, I can attest that acrylic cages clean up easily with a damp towel and regular changing of the tray that slides under the cage itself. If you choose an acrylic cage for your pet, make sure it has numerous ventilation holes drilled in its walls to allow for adequate air circulation. Be particularly careful about not leaving your budgie in direct sunlight if you choose to house it in an acrylic cage, since these cages can get warm rather quickly and your bird could become overheated. (Budgies in wire cages shouldn't be left in direct sunlight either, as they can overheat, too.)

Cage Considerations

Your budgie will spend much of its time in its cage, so make this environment as stimulating, safe and comfortable as possible. Keep the following things in mind when choosing a good cage for your budgie.

- Make sure the cage is big enough. The dimensions of the cage (height, length and depth) should add up to 60 for a single bird.
- An acrylic cage may mean easier clean-up for the bird owner. Wood or bamboo cages will be quickly destroyed by an eager budgie's beak.
- Make sure the cage door opens easily and stays securely open and closed. Avoid "guillotine-style" doors.
- The cage tray should be regularly shaped and easy to slide in and out. There should be a grille covering the cage floor so you can change the substrate without worrying about the bird's escape.

Living with a Budgie

If you find wooden or bamboo cages during your shopping excursions, reject them immediately unless the wood is lined with wire or wire mesh. A busy budgie beak will make short work of a wooden or bamboo cage, and you'll be left with the problem of finding a new home for your pet! These cages are designed for finches and other songbirds that are less likely to chew on their homes than a budgie.

If you choose a wire cage, examine it carefully before making your final selection. Make sure that the finish is not chipped, bubbled or peeling, because a curious budgie may find the spot and continue removing the finish. This can cause a cage to look old and worn before its time, and some cages may start to rust without their protective finishes. Finally, if your budgie ingests any of the finish, it could become ill.

Reject any cages that have sharp interior wires or wide bar spacing. (Recommended bar spacing for budgies is between 3/8 and 7/16 inch.) Sharp wires could poke your bird, and it could become caught between bars that are slightly wider than recommended, or it could escape through widely spaced bars. Also be aware that some birds may injure themselves on ornate scrollwork that decorates some cages. Finally, make sure the cage you choose has some horizontal bars in it so your budgie will be able to climb the cage walls easier if it wants to exercise.

Cage Door Options

Once you've checked the bar spacing and the overall cage quality, your next concern should be the cage door. Does it open easily for you, yet remain secure enough to keep your bird in its cage when you close the door? Is it wide enough for you to get your hand in and out of the cage comfortably? Will your bird's food bowl or a bowl of bath water fit through it easily? Does the door open up, down or to the side? Some bird owners prefer that their pets have a play porch on a door that opens drawbridge style, while others are happy with doors that open to the side. Watch out for guillotine-style doors that slide up and over the cage entrance, because some budgies have suffered broken legs when the door dropped on them unexpectedly.

Cage Tray Considerations

Next, look at the cage tray. Does it slide in and out of the cage easily? Remember that you will be changing the paper in this tray at least once a day for the rest of your bird's life (about 15 years with good care). Is the tray an odd shape or size? Will paper need to be cut into unusual shapes to fit in it, or will paper towels, newspapers or clean sheets of used computer paper fit easily into it? The easier the tray is to remove and reline, the more likely you will be to change the lining of the tray daily. Can the cage tray be replaced if it becomes damaged and unusable? Ask your pet store staff or the cage manufacturer's customer service department before making your purchase.

A cage that has an easily removable, regularly shaped tray will be easier to clean and reline daily.

While we're in the cage tray, let me briefly address cage substrate or what to put in the cage tray. I recommend clean black-and-white newsprint, paper towels or clean sheets of used computer printer paper. Sand, ground corncobs or walnut shells may be sold by your pet supply store, but I don't recommend these as cage flooring materials because they tend to make owners lazy in their cage cleaning habits. These materials tend to hide feces and discarded food quite well. This can cause a bird owner to forget to change the cage tray on the principle that if it doesn't look dirty, it must not be dirty. This line of thinking can set up a thriving, robust colony of bacteria in the bottom of your bird's cage, which can lead to a sick bird if you're not careful. Newsprint and other paper products don't hide the dirt; in fact, they seem to enhance it and draw attention to it, which leads conscientious bird owners to keep their pets' homes scrupulously clean.

On a related note, you may see sandpaper or "gravel paper" sold in some pet stores as a cage tray liner. This product is supposed to provide a budgie with an opportunity to ingest grit, which is purported to help aid its digestion by providing coarse grinding material that will help break up food in the bird's gizzard. The problem is that experts are unable to agree on just how much grit a pet bird needs. Many British avicultural books advocate offering a budgie regular supplements of grit, while American budgie fanciers are less generous with their offerings because some budgies have overeaten grit that is offered to them. This causes impacted crops, a serious condition that requires immediate veterinary attention. Additionally, if a bird stands on rough sandpaper when it's on the cage floor, it could become prone to infections and other foot problems from the rough surface of the paper. For your budgie's health, please don't use these gravel-coated papers.

A sheet, towel or blanket makes an effective cage cover.

Cage Floor

Finally, check the floor of the cage you've chosen. Does it have a grille that will keep your bird out of the debris that falls to the bottom of the cage, such as feces, seed hulls, molted feathers and discarded food? To ensure your pet's long-term good health, it's best to have a grille between your curious pet and the remains of its day in the cage tray. Also, it's easier to keep your budgie in its cage while you're cleaning the cage tray if there's a grille between the cage and the tray.

The Cage Cover

One important, but sometimes overlooked, accessory is the cage cover. Be sure that you have something to cover your budgie's cage with when it's time to put your pet to sleep each night. The act of covering the cage seems to calm many pet birds and convince them that it's really time to go to bed although they may hear the sounds of an active family evening in the background.

You can purchase a cage cover, or you can use an old sheet, blanket or towel that is clean and free of holes. Be aware that some birds like to chew on their cage covers through the cage bars. If your bird does this, replace the cover when it becomes too tattered to do its job effectively. Replacing a well-chewed cover will also help keep your bird from becoming entangled in the cover or caught in a ragged clump of threads. Some birds have injured themselves quite severely by being caught in a worn cage cover, so help keep your pet safe from this hazard.

Where To Put the Cage

Now that you've picked the perfect cage for your pet, where will you put it in your home? Your budgie will be happiest when it can feel like it's part of the family, so the living room, family room or dining room may be among the best places for your bird. If your budgie is a child's pet, it may do well living in its young owner's room. (Parents should still check on the budgie, though, to ensure that it's being fed and watered regularly and that its cage is clean.) Whatever room you choose, keep the cage out of

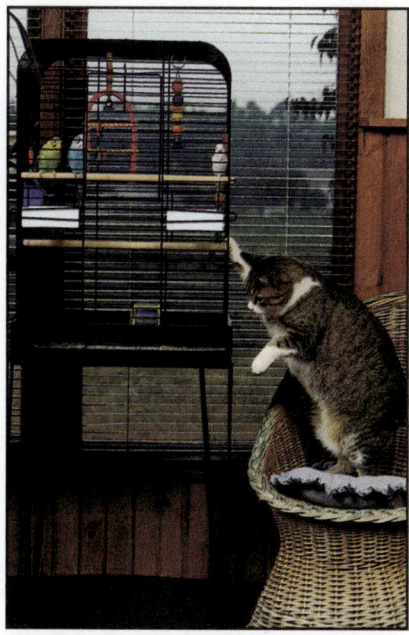

This is an example of a very stressful cage situation. Keep your budgie's cage away from windows and out of reach of curious cats.

direct sunlight and make sure that the cage is placed up against a solid wall so that your budgie doesn't become stressed by feeling that its home is exposed on all sides.

Avoid keeping your budgie in the bathroom or kitchen, though, because sudden temperature fluctuations or fumes from cleaning products used in those rooms could harm your pet. Another spot to avoid is a busy hall or entryway, because the activity level in these spots may be too much for your pet.

Additional Supplies

Along with the perfect-sized cage in the ideal location in your home, your pet will need a few cage accessories. These include food and water dishes, perches and toys.

Food and Water Dishes

When selecting dishes for your budgie, be sure to pick up several sets so that mealtime cleanups are quick and easy. Choose only uncovered dishes for your pet's food and water because budgies are often reluctant to stick their heads into hooded feeders to eat. Some have even starved to death rather than eat from a covered dish. Be sure to check your bird's seed dish daily to make sure that it has seeds, rather than just empty seed hulls in the dish, and refill when necessary.

Perches

When choosing perches for your pet's cage, try to buy two different diameters or materials so your bird's feet won't get tired of standing on the same-sized perch of the same material day after day. Think of how tired your feet would feel if you stood on a piece of wood in your bare feet all day, then imagine how it would feel to stand on that piece of wood barefoot every day for ten or fifteen years. Sounds pretty uncomfortable, doesn't it? That's basically what your bird has to look forward to if you don't vary its perching choices.

The recommended diameter for budgie perches is 1/2 inch, so try to buy one perch that's this size and one that is slightly larger (5/8 inch, for example) to give your pet a chance to stretch its foot muscles. Birds spend almost all of their lives standing, so keeping their feet healthy is important. Also, avian foot problems, such as bumblefoot or pressure sores on the soles of the feet, are much easier to prevent than they are to treat after they've become a problem.

When you walk down the bird-care aisle at your local pet store, you'll probably notice that a variety of perch materials are available to bird owners. Along with the traditional wooden dowels are manzanita branches, PVC tubes, rope perches, and terra cotta or concrete grooming perches. Each has its advantages.

Manzanita offers birds varied diameters on the same perch, along with chewing possibilities, while PVC is pretty indestructible. (Make sure any PVC perches you offer your bird have been scuffed slightly with sandpaper to improve traction.) Rope perches also offer varied diameter and a softer perching surface than wood or plastic, and terra cotta and concrete provide slightly abrasive surfaces that birds can use to groom their beaks without severely damaging the skin on their feet in the process. Some bird owners have reported that their pets have suffered foot abrasions with these perches, however; watch your budgie carefully for signs of sore feet (signs may include an inability to perch or climb, favoring a foot or raw, sore skin on the feet) if you choose to use these perches in your pet's cage. If your bird shows signs of lameness, remove the abrasive perches immediately and arrange for your avian veterinarian to examine your bird.

A perch placed toward the top of the cage will serve as a sleeping roost for your budgie.

To further help your bird avoid foot problems, do not use sandpaper covers on its perches. These sleeves, touted as nail trimming devices, really do little to trim a parrot's nails because birds don't usually drag their nails along their perches. What the sandpaper perch covers are good at doing, though, is abrading the surface of your budgie's feet, which can leave them vulnerable to infections and can make movement painful.

When placing perches in your budgie's cage, try to vary the heights slightly so your bird has different "levels" in its cage. Don't place any perches over food or water dishes, because birds can and will contaminate food or water by defecating in it. Finally, place one perch higher than the rest for a nighttime sleeping roost. Budgies and other parrots like to sleep on the highest point they can find to perch, so please provide this security to your pet.

Because perches can sometimes double as chew toys, don't be alarmed if your budgie suddenly seems to become a feathered termite. It may need more chew toys in its cage, or it may just like destroying perches. In either case, be prepared to make many trips to your pet store for replacement toys and perches, and be glad that you have a healthy, well-adjusted pet that likes to play.

Choosing the Right Toys

When selecting toys for your pet, keep a few safety tips in mind.

SIZE

First, is the toy the right size for your bird? Large toys can be intimidating to small birds, which makes the birds less likely to play with them. On the other end of the spectrum, larger parrots can easily destroy toys designed for smaller birds, and they can sometimes injure themselves severely in the process.

SAFETY

Next, is the toy safe? Good choices include sturdy wooden toys (either undyed or painted with bird-safe vegetable dye or food coloring) strung on closed-link chains or vegetable-tanned leather thongs, and rope toys. If you purchase rope toys for your budgie, make sure its nails are trimmed regularly to prevent them from snagging in the rope, and discard the toy when it becomes frayed to prevent accidents.

Unsafe items to watch out for are brittle plastic toys that can be shattered into fragments easily by a budgie's busy beak, lead-weighted toys that can be cracked open to expose the dangerous lead to curious birds, loose link chains that can catch toenails or beaks, ring toys that are too small to climb through safely, or jingle-type bells that can trap toes, tongues or beaks.

A homemade toy of toilet paper tubes will delight your budgie.

Introducing Toys

Mirrors are found on many budgie toys, and most birds are fascinated with and enamored of that handsome pet in the reflection. Some birds become so infatuated with "the other bird" that they seem to lose interest in their owners, so you might want to want until your budgie is settled in its surroundings and comfortable with you before adding a mirrored toy to its cage.

Noise as Company

Earlier, I mentioned the importance of having a radio or television on for your budgie if you leave it home alone for long periods of time. Although budgies have been kept as pets for about 150 years, they may still instinctively harken back to their wild roots at times. In the grasslands of Australia as in the jungles of Latin America and Africa, silence usually indicates a predator in the area, which can raise a bird's stress level. Because you don't want a stressed-out pet, please leave a radio or television on for your budgie if you will be away so that it will have some background noise and some variety in its daily routine. Some budgies may even learn the words to commercial jingles they hear on the radio or TV!

The Playgym

Although your budgie will spend quite a bit of time in its cage, it will also need time out of its cage to exercise and enjoy a change of scenery. A playgym can be just what your budgie needs to keep it physically and mentally active.

If you visit a large pet store or bird specialty store, or look through the pages of any pet bird hobbyist magazine, you will see a variety of playgyms on display. You can choose a complicated gym with a series of ladders, swings, perches and toys, or you can purchase a simple T-stand that has a place for food and water bowls and an eyescrew or two from which you can hang toys. If you're really handy with tools, you can even construct a gym to your budgie's size and playing specifications.

As with the cage, the location of your budgie's playgym will be a consideration. You will want the gym placed in a secure location in your home that is safe from other curious pets, ceiling fans, open windows and other household hazards. You will also want the gym to be in a spot frequented by your family, so your bird will have company and supervision while it plays.

A playgym will help to keep your budgie physically and mentally stimulated.

chapter

4

Feeding Your Budgie

People do not live by bread alone, and birds can't prosper on a diet of seeds and water. Think how dull and unhealthy a one-item diet would be for you—it isn't any more interesting for your budgie.

Poor diet also causes a number of health problems (respiratory infections, poor feather condition, flaky skin, reproductive problems, to name a few) and is one of the main reasons some budgies live fairly short lives. Let's look again at my childhood pet, who ate basically a seed-and-water diet and lived about five years. If we had offered him a more varied diet, Charlie could have lived three times that long.

A Healthy Diet

Here's what the Association of Avian Veterinarians recommends as a healthy budgie diet: 50 percent seed, grain and legumes; 45 percent dark green or dark orange vegetables and fruits; and 5 percent meat (well cooked, please), eggs (also well cooked) or dairy products. We'll look at each part of this diet in a little more detail in just a moment.

Whatever healthy fresh foods you offer your budgie, be sure to remove any leftover food from the cage promptly to prevent spoilage and to help keep your bird healthy. Ideally, you should change the food in your bird's cage every two to four hours (about every thirty minutes in warm weather), so a budgie should be all right with a tray of food to pick through in the morning, another to select from during the afternoon and a third fresh salad to nibble on for dinner.

Seeds and Grains

First, the seeds, grain and legumes portion of your budgie's diet can include clean, fresh seed from your local pet supply store. Give your pet its seeds in a clean, dry dish, and check the dish daily to ensure your budgie has enough food. Don't just look in the dish, but actually

Millet sprays are a budgie favorite, but offer them sparingly because they are high in fat.

remove it from the cage and blow lightly into the dish (you might want to do this over the kitchen sink or the trash can) to remove seed hulls. Budgies are notorious for giving the impression that they have enough food. Because they are such neat eaters and drop the used hulls right back in their dishes, they can often fool you.

One foodstuff that is very popular with budgies is millet, especially millet sprays. These golden sprays are part treat and part toy. Offer your budgie this treat sparingly, however, your teeth. Although you may see birds doing this on television or in pictures in a magazine and think that it's a cute trick, it's really unsafe for your bird's health and well-being.

Enticing the Older Budgie

If you've adopted an older budgie that eats primarily seeds, try offering your bird some of the fruits and vegetables that are popular with many parrots, such as apple slices, grapes or corn. You can offer a small slice of apple that you've dipped in seeds, a halved grape or some fresh corn kernels (offering a budgie-sized slice of corn on the cob is also an option). Although these fruits and vegetables are not as rich in important vitamins as their dark green or dark orange counterparts, they can help bridge the gap between seeds and a more varied diet for fussy eaters. To ease the stress of relocating to your home, try to feed your budgie a diet as close to the one it ate in its previous home. To help your bird adjust even faster, you may want to sprinkle some food on the cage floor, because budgies sometimes revert to their natural ground-feeding habits in times of stress.

The Pelleted Diet Option

Just what is a pellet anyway, you're probably thinking. Don't birds just eat seeds? While seeds are an important part of many birds' diets, some budgie owners prefer to feed their pets a pelleted diet rather than a mixture of seeds, vegetables, fruits and healthful table food.

Pelleted diets are created by mixing a variety of healthful ingredients into a mash and then forcing (or extruding) the hot mixture through a machine to form various shapes. Some pelleted diets have colors and flavors added, while others are fairly plain. These formulated diets provide more balanced nutrition for your pet bird in an easy-to-serve form that reduces the amount of wasted food and eliminates the

> **Your Budgie's Beak**
>
> Because budgies eat primarily seeds and other plant materials (in the wild, some budgies have been seen eating the seeds of 21 different species of grasses), their beaks have developed into efficient little seed crackers. Notice the underside of your bird's upper beak if you can. It has tiny ridges in it that help your budgie hold and crack seeds more easily.

chance for a bird to pick through a smorgasbord of healthful foods to find its favorites and reject the foods it isn't particularly fond of. Some budgies accept pelleted diets quickly, while others require some persuading.

If your budgie seems a bit finicky about trying pellets, you may have to make it believe that you enjoy pellets as a snack. Really play up your apparent enjoyment of this new food because it will pique your budgie's curiosity and make the pellets exceedingly interesting to your pet.

If you have another bird in the house that already eats a pelleted diet, place your budgie's cage where it can watch the other bird enjoy its pellets. Before long, your budgie will be playing "follow the leader" right to the food bowl. Finally, you may want to roll a favorite treat, such as a damp broccoli floret or an apple slice, in pellets and offer this decorated piece of produce to your pet.

Whatever you do, don't starve your bird into trying a new food. Offer a variety of new foods consistently, along with familiar favorites. This will ensure that your bird is eating and will also encourage it to try new foods. Don't be discouraged if your budgie doesn't dive right in to a new food. Be patient, keep offering new foods to your bird and praise it enthusiastically when it is brave enough to sample something new!

A pelleted diet offers a full complement of vitamins and minerals. You may have to be patient and ingenious to get your budgie to accept it.

Grit

As a new bird owner, you may hear a lot of talk about the importance of grit in your bird's diet. Birds use grit in their gizzards to grind their food, much as we use our teeth. How much grit birds need and how often it should be offered to them is a source of contention among avian veterinarians and bird breeders. Some will tell you birds need grit regularly, while others will advise against it. If your budgie's breeder and your avian veterinarian think your bird requires grit, offer it sparingly (only about a pinch every few weeks). Do not offer it daily, and do not provide your budgie with a separate dish of grit because some birds will overeat the grit and suffer dangerous crop impactions as a result.

Supplements

You may also be concerned if your bird is receiving adequate amounts of vitamins and minerals in its diet. This is of particular concern if your budgie is eating a seed-based diet. Budgies on pelleted or formulated diets should have all their vitamin and mineral needs met with these special diets, so additional supplements are unnecessary. If your budgie's diet is mainly seeds, however, you may want to sprinkle a good-quality vitamin-and-mineral powder onto your pet's fresh foods, where it has the best chance of sticking to the food and being eaten. Vitamin-enriched seed diets may provide some supplementation, but some of them add the vitamins and minerals to the seed hull, which your pet will remove and discard while it's eating. Avoid adding vitamin and mineral supplements to your budgie's water dish, because they can act as a growth medium for bacteria. They may also cause the water to taste different to your bird, which could discourage it from drinking.

chapter

5

Grooming a
Budgie

Your budgie has several grooming needs. It must be able to bathe regularly, and it will need to have its nails and flight feathers trimmed periodically to ensure its safety.

Although some people would say that a budgie's beak also needs trimming, I would argue that a healthy bird that has enough chew toys seems to do a remarkable job of keeping its beak trimmed. If your budgie's beak becomes overgrown, though, please consult your avian veterinarian. A parrot's beak contains a surprising number of blood vessels, so beak trimming is best left to the experts. Also, a suddenly overgrown beak may indicate that your bird is suffering from liver damage, a virus or scaly mites, all of which require veterinary care.

A healthy bird with plenty of chew toys is unlikely to need a beak trim. If you think your budgie does, consult your veterinarian.

Preening

This is your one of your budgie's ways of keeping itself well-groomed. You will notice it ruffling and straightening its feathers each day. It will also take oil from the gland at the base of its tail and spread it on the rest of its feathers, so don't be concerned if you see your budgie apparently pecking or biting at its tail. Preening, combined with your assistance in bathing, nail clipping and wing clipping will keep your budgie in top shape.

Bathing Your Budgie

You can bathe your budgie in a variety of ways. You can mist it lightly with a clean spray bottle filled with warm water only, or you can allow it to bathe in the kitchen or bathroom sink under a slow stream of water. Many budgies prefer to bathe in their cages, either in a small flat saucer of warm water, a plastic budgie bathtub or an enclosed bird bath that you can purchase in your local pet

Preening is the way your bird naturally grooms itself.

store. Bathing is important to birds to help them keep their feathers clean and healthy, so don't deny your pet the chance to bathe!

Unless your budgie has gotten itself into oil, paint, wax or some other substance that elbow grease alone won't remove and that could harm its feathers, it will not require soap as part of its bath. Under routine conditions, soaps and detergents can damage a bird's feathers by removing beneficial oils, so hold the shampoo during your budgie's normal clean-up routine!

Let your bird bathe early in the day so it has an opportunity to let its feathers dry completely during the day. In cooler weather, you may want help the process along by drying your budgie off with a blow dryer—set the blow dryer on low and keep it moving. Your budgie may soon learn that drying off is the most enjoyable part of its bath!

Budgies like to bathe in any number of ways. This one is enjoying its bath in a special budgie bathtub.

Nail Trimming

Trimming your budgie's nails is a fairly simple procedure. Budgies and other parrots need their nails clipped occasionally to prevent the nails from catching on toys or perches and injuring themselves. Unlike some of the larger parrots, budgie nails are light in color, which makes it easier for owners to see where the nail stops and the blood and blood supply (or quick) begins. In budgies, the quick is generally seen as a pink color inside the nail.

You will need to remove only tiny portions of the nail to keep your budgie's claws trimmed. Generally, a good guideline to follow is to only remove the hook on each nail, and to do this in the smallest increments possible. Stop well before you reach the quick. If you do happen to cut the nail short enough to make it bleed, apply cornstarch or flour, followed by direct pressure, to stop the bleeding.

Wing Trimming

The goal of a properly done wing trim is to prevent your pet from flying away or flying into a window, mirror or wall while it's out of its cage. An added benefit of trimming your pet's wings is that its inability to fly well will make it more dependent on you for transportation, which should make it easier to handle. However, the bird still needs enough wing feathers so that it can glide safely to the ground if it is startled and takes flight from its cagetop or playgym.

Because this is a delicate procedure, it is best to enlist the help of your avian veterinarian, at least the first time. Wing trimming is a task that must be performed carefully to avoid injuring your pet. If you feel up to the task, ask your vet for instructions on how to do the procedure thereafter by yourself.

To trim the right length off your budgie's nails, cut only the hook at the end of each nail.

Molting

At least once a year, your budgie will lose its feathers. Don't be alarmed, because this is a normal process called molting. I say at least once because many pet birds seem to be in a perpetual molt, with feathers falling out and coming in throughout the summer.

You can consider your bird in molting season when you see a lot of whole feathers in the bottom of the cage and you notice that your bird seems to have broken out in a rash of stubbly little aglets (that look like those plastic tips on the ends of your shoelaces). These are the feather sheaths that help new pinfeathers break through the skin, and they are made of keratin (the same material that makes up our fingernails). The sheaths helps protect growing feathers from damage until the feather completes its growth cycle.

You may notice that your budgie is a little more irritable during the molt; this is to be expected. Think about how you would feel if you had all these itchy new feathers coming in all of a sudden. However, your bird may actively seek out more time with you during the molt because owners are handy to have around when a budgie has an itch on the top of its head that it can't quite scratch! (Scratch these new feathers gently because some of them may still be growing in and may be sensitive to the touch.) Some birds may benefit from special conditioning foods during the molt; check with your avian veterinarian to see if your bird is a candidate for these foods.

> **Grooming Tips**
>
> Groom your pet in a quiet, well-lit place.
>
> Have all the necessary grooming supplies on hand before you begin.
>
> Make sure you have styptic powder on hand.
>
> Check wings and toenails regularly to see if they need retrimming.

Be particularly alert after a molt, because your bird will have a whole new crop of flight feathers that need attention. You'll be able to tell when your budgie is due for a trim when it starts becoming bolder in its flying attempts. Right after a wing trim, a budgie generally tries to fly and finds it's unsuccessful at the attempt. It will keep trying, though, and may surprise you one day with a fairly good glide across its cage or from its playgym. If this happens, call your vet and get those wings trimmed immediately. If you don't, the section that follows on finding lost birds may have more meaning that you can imagine.

If Your Bird Escapes

As we discuss wing trimming, it is as good a time as any to discuss the possibility of your bird escaping. One of the most common accidents that befalls bird owners is that a fully flighted bird escapes through an open door or window. Just because your bird has never flown before or shown any interest in leaving its cage doesn't mean that it can't fly or that it won't become disoriented once it's outside.

How can you prevent your bird from becoming lost? First, make sure its wings are safely trimmed at regular intervals. Be sure to trim both wings evenly and remember to trim wings after your bird has molted.

Next, be sure your bird's cage door locks securely and that its cage tray cannot come loose if the cage is knocked over or dropped accidentally. Also be sure that all your window screens fit securely and are free from tears and large holes. Keep all window screens and patio doors closed when your bird is at liberty. Finally, don't ever go outside with your bird on your shoulder.

If, despite your best efforts, your bird should escape, you must act quickly for the best chance of recovering your pet. Here are some things to keep in mind:

If your bird does fly away, use an open, inviting cage, and a tape of the bird's voice played outside to lure it home.

Have an audiotape of your bird's voice and a portable tape recorder available to lure your bird back home.

Place your bird's cage in an area when your bird is likely to see it, such as on a deck or patio. Put lots of treats and food on the floor of the cage to tempt your pet back into its home.

Use another caged bird to attract your budgie's attention.

Alert your avian veterinarian's office that your bird has escaped. Also let the local humane society and other veterinary offices in your area know.

Post fliers in your neighborhood describing your bird. Offer a reward and include your phone number.

Don't give up hope.

chapter

6

Your Budgie's Physical Health

Avian Anatomy

If you think your body doesn't have much in common with your pet budgie's, you'd be wrong. You both have skin; skeletons; respiratory, cardiovascular, digestive, excretory and nervous systems; and sensory organs, although the various systems function in slightly different ways.

Skin

Your budgie's skin is probably pretty difficult to see since your pet has so many feathers. If you part the feathers carefully, though, you can see your pet's thin, transparent skin and the muscles beneath it. Modified skin cells help make up your bird's beak, cere, claws and the scales on its feet and legs.

Digestive System

To keep this energy-efficient machine (your bird's body) running requires fuel (or food). This is where your bird's digestive system comes in. One of the main functions of the digestive system is to provide the fuel that maintains your bird's body temperature. A bird's body temperature is higher than a human's. The first time I bird-sat for friends, I worried about their cockatoo's seemingly hot feet. After another bird owner told me that birds have higher temperatures than people, I stopped worrying.

Your budgie's digestive system begins with its **beak.** The size and shape of a bird's beak depends on its food-gathering needs. Compare and contrast the sharp, pointed beak of an eagle or the elongated bill of a hummingbird with the small, hooked beak of your budgie.

A parrot's mouth works a little differently than a mammal's. Parrots don't have saliva to help break down and move their food around like we do. Also, their taste buds are contained in the roofs of their mouths. Because they have few taste buds, experts think that a parrot's sense of taste is poorly developed.

After the food leaves your bird's mouth, it travels down the **esophagus,** where it is moistened. The food then travels to the **crop,** where it is moistened further and is supplied in small increments to the bird's stomach.

After the food leaves the crop, it travels through the **proventriculus,** where digestive juices are added, to the **gizzard,** where the food is broken down into even smaller pieces. The food then travels to the **small intestine,** where nutrients are absorbed into the bloodstream. Anything that's leftover then travels through the large intestine to the **cloaca,** which is the common chamber that collects wastes before they leave the bird's body through the vent. The whole process from mouth to vent usually takes only a few hours, which is why you may notice that your bird leaves frequent, small droppings in its cage.

Along with the solid waste created by the digestive system, your budgie's kidneys create urine, which is then transported through ureters to the cloaca for excretion. Unlike a mammal, a bird does not have a bladder or a urethra.

Nervous System

Your budgie's nervous system is very similar to your own. Both are made up of the brain, the spinal cord and countless nerves throughout the body that transmit messages to and from the brain.

Now that we've examined some of the similarities between avian and human anatomy, let's stop and look at some of the unusual anatomical features birds have. The first feature I'd like to discuss is probably one of the reasons you're attracted to birds: feathers. Birds are the only animals that have feathers, which serve several purposes. Feathers help birds fly, they keep birds warm, they attract the attention of potential mates, and they help scare away predators.

Feathers

Did you know that your budgie has between 2,000 and 3,000 feathers on its body? These feathers grow from follicles that are arranged in rows known as pterylae. The unfeathered patches of bare skin on your budgie's body are called apteria.

A feather is a remarkably designed creation. The base of the feather shaft, which fits into the bird's skin, is called the quill. It is light and hollow, but remarkably tough. The upper part of the feather shaft is called the rachis. From it branch the barbs and barbules (smaller barbs) that make up most of the feather. The barbs and barbules have small hooks on them that enable the different parts of the feather to interlock like Velcro and form the feather's vane or web.

Birds have several different types of feathers on their bodies. **Contour feathers** are the colorful outer feathers on a bird's body and wings. Many birds have an undercoating of down feathers that help keep them warm. **Semiplume feathers** are found on a bird's beak, nares (nostrils) and eyelids.

A bird's flight feathers can be classified into one of two types. **Primary flight feathers** are the large wing feathers that push a bird forward during flight. They are also the ones that need clipping. **Secondary flight feathers** are found on the inner wing, and they help support the bird in flight. Primary and secondary wing feathers can operate independently of each other. The bird's tail feathers also assist in flight by acting as a brake and a rudder to make steering easier.

Feather colors are determined by combinations of pigment in the outer keratin layer and in the interior structure of the feather.

To keep their feathers in good condition, healthy birds will spend a great deal of time fluffing their feathers and preening them. You may see your budgie seeming to pick at the base of its tail on the topside. This is a normal behavior in which the bird removes oil from the preen gland and spreads it on its feathers. The oil also helps prevent skin infections and waterproofs the feathers.

Your budgie has between 2,000 and 3,000 feathers on its body.

Sometimes pet birds will develop white lines or small holes on the large feathers of their wings and tails. These lines or holes are referred to as "stress bars" or "stress lines" and result from the bird being under stress as the feathers were developing. If you notice stress bars on your budgie's feathers, discuss them with your avian veterinarian.

Budgie Senses

Sight

Not surprisingly, since flight requires it, birds have quite a well-developed sense of sight. They can see detail and they can discern colors. Be aware of this when selecting cage accessories for your pet, because some budgies react to a change in the color of their food dishes. Some seem excited by a different color bowl, while others act fearful of the new item.

Because their eyes are located on the sides of their heads, most pet birds rely on monocular vision, which means that they use each eye independent of the other. If a bird really wants to study an object, you will often see it tilt its head to one side and examine the object with just one eye. Birds aren't really able to move their eyes around very much, but they compensate for this by having highly mobile necks that allow them to turn their heads about 180 degrees.

Like cats and dogs, birds have third eyelids called nictitating membranes that you will sometimes see flick briefly across your budgie's eye. The purpose of this membrane is to keep the eyeball moist and clean. If you see your budgie's nictitating membrane for more than a brief second, please contact your avian veterinarian for an evaluation.

You have probably noticed that your bird lacks eyelashes. In their place are small feathers called semiplumes that help keep dirt and dust out of the bird's eyeball.

Hearing

You may be wondering where your budgie's ears are. Look carefully under the feathers behind and below each eye to find them. The ears are the somewhat large holes in the sides of your budgie's head. Budgies have about the same ability to distinguish sound waves and determine the location of the sound as people do, but birds seem to be less sensitive to higher and lower pitches than their owners.

Taste and Smell

Birds seem to have poorly developed senses of smell and taste because smells often dissipate quickly in the air (where flying birds spend their time) and because birds have a small number of taste buds in their mouths.

Touch

The final sense we relate to, touch, is well-developed in parrots. Parrots use their feet and their mouths to touch their surroundings (young birds particularly seem to "mouth" everything they can get their beaks on), to play and to determine what is safe to perch on or chew on and what's good to eat.

Along with their tactile uses, a parrot's feet also have an unusual design compared to other caged birds. Look at your budgie's feet, and compare them to those of a finch, softbill or canary. Do you notice that, unlike a finch or canary, two of your budgie's toes point forward and two point backward? This two toes forward and two toes back arrangement is called zygodactyl, and it allows a parrot to climb up and down, and around in trees easily. Some larger parrots also use their feet to hold food or to play with toys.

Like all parrots, budgies have four toes—two pointing forward and two pointing backward.

Visiting the Veterinarian

With good care, a budgerigar can live up to eighteen years, although the average life span of these small parrots is about one-third of that, or six years. One of the reasons budgies don't live longer is that their owners may be reluctant to take their pets to the veterinarian. Some people don't want to pay veterinary bills on such "inexpensive" birds.

Choosing a Veterinarian

As a caring owner, you want your bird to have good care and the best chance at living a long, healthy life. To that end, you will need to locate a veterinarian who understands the special medical needs of birds and one with whom you can establish a good working relationship. The best time to do this is when you first bring your budgie home from the breeder or pet store. If possible, arrange to visit your veterinarian's office on your way home from the breeder or store.

This is particularly important if you have other birds at home, because you don't want to endanger the health of your existing flock or your new pet.

If you don't know an avian veterinarian in your area, ask the person you bought your budgie from where he or she takes his or her birds. (Breeders and bird stores usually have avian veterinarians on whom they depend.) Talk to other bird owners you know and find out who they take their pets to, or call bird clubs in your area for referrals.

If you have no bird-owning friends or can't locate a bird club, your next best bet is the yellow pages. Read the advertisements for veterinarians carefully, and try to find one who specializes in birds. Many veterinarians who have an interest in treating birds will join the Association of Avian Veterinarians and advertise themselves as members of this organization. Some veterinarians have taken and passed a special examination that entitles them to call themselves avian specialists.

Once you've received your recommendations or found likely candidates in the telephone book, start calling the veterinary offices. Ask the receptionist how many birds the doctor sees in a week or month, how much an office visit costs, and what payment options are available (cash, credit card, check or time payments). You can also inquire if the doctor keeps birds as his or her personal pets.

If you like the answers you receive from the receptionist, make an appointment for your budgie to be evaluated. (If you don't,

> ### Signs of Illness
>
> To help your veterinarian and to keep your pet from suffering long-term health risks, keep a close eye on its daily activities and appearance. If something suddenly changes in the way your bird looks or acts, contact your veterinarian immediately. Birds naturally hide signs of illness to protect themselves from predators, so by the time a bird looks or acts sick, it may already be dangerously ill.
>
> Some signs of illness include:
>
> - a fluffed-up appearance
> - a loss of appetite
> - sleeping all the time
> - a change in the appearance or number of droppings
> - weight loss
> - listlessness
> - drooping wings
> - lameness
> - partially eaten food stuck to the bird's face or food that has been regurgitated onto the cage floor
> - labored breathing, with or without tail bobbing
> - runny eyes or nose
> - the bird stops talking or singing
>
> If your bird shows any of these signs, please contact your veterinarian's office immediately.

of course, move on to the next name on your list.) Make a list of any questions you want to ask the doctor regarding diet, how often your bird's wings and nails should be clipped or how often you should bring the bird in for an examination.

Plan to arrive a little early for your first appointment because you will be asked to fill out a patient information form. This form will ask you for your bird's name, its age and sex, the length of time you have owned it, your name, address and telephone number, your preferred method of paying for veterinary services, how you heard about the veterinary office, and the name and address of a friend the veterinary office can contact in case of emergency. The form may also ask you to express your opinion on the amount of money you would spend on your pet in an emergency, because this can help the doctor know what kind of treatment to recommend in such instances.

Medicating Your Budgie

Most bird owners are faced with the prospect of medicating their pets at some point in the birds' lives, and many are unsure if they can complete the task without hurting their pets. If you have to medicate your pet, your avian veterinarian or veterinary technician should explain the process to you. In the course of the explanation, you should find out how you will be administering the medication, how much of a given drug you will be giving your bird, how often the bird needs the medication and how long the entire course of treatment will last.

If you find (as I often have) that you've forgotten one or more of these steps after you arrive home, call your vet's office for clarification to ensure that your bird receives the follow-up care from you that it needs.

Budgie Health Concerns

Although budgies are generally hardy birds, they are prone to a few health problems, including scaly face, goiter, gout, obesity and lipomas. They, like all birds, can also suffer from respiratory problems and other conditions that result from a vitamin-A deficiency, especially if they consume diets that are high in seeds and low in vitamin-A-rich foods. Vitamin-A deficiency can be prevented by feeding a varied, healthy diet.

Scaly Face

Scaly face is a condition caused by the *Knemidokoptes* mite, a tiny relative of the spider that likes to burrow into the top layers of a budgie's skin around its cere, eyelids, vent or legs. This burrowing leaves white crusts on the bird's cere or the corners of the mouth. If allowed to progress, scaly face can cause lesions on a bird's beak, eyelids, throat, vent, legs and feet. Advanced cases can also cause beak deformation and horny appendages on a bird's face and legs. The leg appendages can interfere with a bird's ability to move its legs and toes.

If your avian veterinarian suspects your budgie has scaly face, he or she will diagnose the condition by examining skin scrapings under a microscope. Although scaly face has the potential to be a serious condition, the good news is that it can be easily treated by a veterinarian using Ivermectin, which will remove the mites and restore the skin to its normal appearance.

Although some over-the-counter remedies are sold to treat scaly face, a veterinarian-supervised course of treatment using Ivermectin will clear up the problem more quickly and easily than using a nonprescription product.

Goiter

Goiter is an enlargement of the thyroid gland in a bird's throat. It is caused by an iodine deficiency and is most often seen in budgies that eat seed-only diets. Symptoms include difficulty in breathing and swallowing, and regurgitation. Your veterinarian can determine if your budgie has a goiter through x-rays and blood tests. Iodine supplements are used to treat the condition.

Gout

Gout is associated with kidney problems. Specifically, gouty birds have kidneys that are unable to remove excess nitrogen from the bird's bloodstream. This causes uric acid and urates to build up in the bird's body or in its joints. The exact cause of gout is unclear at this time, but high levels of dietary sodium or calcium and inadequate fluid intake, may contribute to gout.

Two forms of gout occur: articular gout, which affects a bird's lower leg joints as shiny, cream-colored swellings, and visceral gout, which affects a bird's internal organs and is difficult to diagnose. Articular gout, the type most often seen in budgies, is a painful condition that causes an affected bird to go lame.

Presently, no cure exists for gout. Treatment includes lowering protein levels and increasing the amount of fruits and vegetables in the bird's diet, along with treating any underlying infections that may have an impact on kidney function. Veterinarians may be able to lower a bird's uric acid levels with medication, and they can also prescribe drugs to ease the bird's pain. Padded perches also seem to offer comfort to afflicted birds.

Obesity

Obesity can sometimes be caused by a malfunctioning thyroid gland, but it is most often caused by a bird eating far more calories than it burns in a day. (English budgies seem to be more prone to obesity than their American cousins.) To prevent this from happening to your pet budgie, make sure that it eats a well-balanced diet that is low in oil seeds and nuts (sunflower seeds, millet, peanuts, walnuts) and that it receives ample opportunity to exercise both inside its cage and outside of it while supervised on a playgym.

If your budgie is overweight, you may notice that it has developed a fatty growth, or lipoma, that may impair its ability to fly. Some experts think that these lipomas are linked to a lack of exercise in budgies. The good news is that most lipomas can be removed safely by your veterinarian.

Bumblefoot

Bumblefoot is an infection of the sole of the bird's foot. It can cause redness and inflammation, swelling and lameness. Antibiotics, bandages and surgery may be needed to treat the condition, which can be prevented by keeping a bird's cage clean and feeding it a well-balanced diet.

Giardia

This illness is caused by a protozoan called *Giardia psittaci*. This organism may cause a bird to have loose droppings, lose weight, pick its feathers, lose its appetite and become depressed. Diagnosing this disease can be tricky, because *Giardia* is difficult to detect in a bird's feces. The disease can be spread through contaminated food or water, and birds are not immune to it once they've had it. Your veterinarian can recommend an appropriate medication to treat *Giardia*.

French Moult

This condition causes flight and tail feathers to develop improperly or not develop at all. Researchers believe the disease is caused by polyomavirus, which can be spread through contact with new birds, as well as from feather and fecal dust.

Adult birds can carry polyomavirus but show no signs of the disease. These seemingly healthy birds can pass the virus to young birds that have never been exposed, and these young birds can die from polyomavirus rather quickly. Sick birds can become weak, lose their appetites, bleed beneath the skin, have enlarged abdomens, become paralyzed, regurgitate and have diarrhea. Some birds with polyomavirus suddenly die.

At present, there is no cure, although a vaccine is under development. Protecting your pets against polyomavirus and other diseases is why it's important to quarantine new stock and to take precautions, including showering and changing clothes, before handling your pet when you've gone to other bird owners' homes, to bird marts that have large numbers of birds from different vendors on display or to bird specialty stores with unhealthy stock.

Papilloma

Papillomas are benign tumors that can appear almost anywhere on a bird's skin, including its foot, leg, eyelid or preen gland. If a bird has a papilloma on its cloaca, the bird may appear to have a "wet raspberry" coming out of its vent. These tumors, which are caused by a virus, can appear as small, crusty lesions, or they may be raised growths that have a bumpy texture or small projections.

Many papillomas can be left untreated without harm to the bird, but some must be removed by an avian veterinarian because a bird may pick at the growth and cause it to bleed.

Psittacine Beak and Feather Disease Syndrome (PBFDS)

This virus was first detected in cockatoos and was originally thought to be a cockatoo-specific problem. It has since been determined that more than forty species of parrots, including budgerigars, can contract this disease, which causes a bird's feathers to become pinched or clubbed in appearance. Other symptoms include beak fractures and mouth ulcers. This highly contagious, fatal disease is most common in birds less than three years of age, and there is no cure at present.

Household Hazards

One of the reasons you chose a budgie as a pet is because it's such a curious, active little bird. These traits can lead your pet into all sorts of mischief around your home, some of which can be harmful to your bird.

Where are you sitting as you read this book? On your couch or in a comfortable chair, or are you lounging on your bed? Any of these seemingly safe spots can be harmful to your budgie, especially if your pet plays hide-and-seek under pillows or cushions and is accidentally sat on by an unsuspecting person. Some parrots have caused themselves great harm by getting tangled in seemingly harmless items, such as towels, sheets or cage covers. Keep these things in mind when you let your budgie out of its cage, and never allow it to play outside its cage without supervision. Just like a small child, a budgie must be protected from its own curiosity at all times.

This doesn't mean you shouldn't let your pet out of its cage. On the contrary, all parrots need time out of their cages to maintain physical and mental health. The key to keeping your pet safe and healthy is to watch over it and play with it when it's out of its cage. Both of you will come to enjoy these playtimes greatly.

Some household hazards to be aware of (dangers to budgies are included in parenthesis) include:

- unscreened windows and doors (escape)
- mirrors (collision and injury)
- exposed electrical cords (electrocution if chewed on)
- toxic houseplants (poisoning)
- unattended ashtrays (burns from lit cigarettes or poisoning from ingesting cigarette butts)
- venetian blind cords (hanging)
- sliding glass doors (escape when open/collision and injury when closed)
- ceiling fans (injury)
- open washing machines, dryers, refrigerators, freezers, ovens or dishwashers (entrapment and subsequent death upon use of appliance)
- open toilet bowls (drowning)
- uncovered fish tanks (drowning)
- leaded stained glass items or inlaid jewelry (poisoning)
- uncovered cooking pots on the stove (drowning/scalding/poisoning/burns)
- crayons and permanent markers (poisoning)
- pesticides, rodent killers and snail bait (poisoning)
- untended stove burners (burns)
- candles (burns)
- open trash cans (entrapment)

Budgie-proofing your home is akin to baby-proofing it. If you consider the fact that your budgie will be intellectually and emotionally a perpetual two year old, you'll have some idea of the responsibility you must be willing to accept when you adopt your pet.

The dangers don't stop with the furniture and accessories. A plethora of fumes can overpower your pet, too, such as those from cigarettes, air fresheners, insecticides, bleach, shoe polish, oven cleaners, kerosene, lighter fluid, model and instant glues, active self-cleaning ovens, hairspray, overheated nonstick cookware, paint thinner, bathroom cleaners or nail polish remover. Try to keep your pet away from anything that has a strong chemical odor, and be sure to apply makeup and hair care products far away from your budgie.

Budgie First Aid

Sometimes your pet will get itself into a situation that will require quick thinking and even quicker action on your part to help save your bird from serious injury or death. Knowing some basic first aid techniques may prove useful in these situations.

Before we get into the specific techniques, make sure you have your bird owner's first aid kit (see sidebar in this chapter for information on what to include).

In *The Complete Bird Owner's Handbook,* veterinarian Gary Gallerstein offers the following advice to bird owners whose birds need urgent care:

No matter what the situation, there are a few things to keep in mind when facing a medical emergency with your pet. First, keep as calm as possible because your bird is already excited enough from being injured, and you getting excited won't help your pet get well. Next, stop any bleeding, keep the bird warm and minimize handling it.

Aloe vera is a safe plant for budgies.

After you've stabilized your pet, call your veterinarian's office for further instructions. Tell them "This is an emergency" and that your bird has had an accident. Describe what happened to your pet as clearly and calmly as you can. Listen carefully to the instructions you are given and follow them. Finally, transport your bird to the vet's office as quickly and safely as you can.

Here are some urgent medical situations that bird owners are likely to encounter, the reason that they are medical emergencies, the signs and symptoms your bird might show and the recommended treatments for the problem.

Animal Bites

Infections can develop from bacteria on the biting animal's teeth and/or claws. Also, a bird's internal organs can be damaged by the bite. Sometimes the bite marks can be seen, but often the bird shows few, if any, signs of injury.

Call your veterinarian's office and transport the bird there immediately. Treatment for shock and antibiotics are often the course of action veterinarians take to save birds that have been bitten.

Beak Injury

A bird needs both its upper and lower beak (also called the upper and lower mandible) to eat and preen properly. Infections can also set in rather quickly if a beak is fractured or punctured.

Plants to Look Out For

Even common houseplants can pose a threat to your pet's health. Here are some plants that are considered poisonous to budgies:

- amaryllis
- calla lily
- daffodil
- dieffenbachia
- English ivy
- foxglove
- holly
- lily-of-the-valley
- mistletoe
- rhubarb

What's a budgie owner to do? Are there any safe plants that you can keep in your home without endangering your feathered friend? Fortunately, yes, there are.

Some plants that are considered safe for bird owners to have in their homes include:

- African violets
- aloe
- burro's tail
- Christmas cactus
- edible fig
- ferns
- gardenia
- grape ivy

An obvious symptom is bleeding from the beak. This often occurs after the bird flies into a windowpane or mirror, or if it has a run-in with an operational ceiling fan. The beak may also be cracked or damaged in which case portions of the beak may be missing.

Control bleeding. Keep bird calm and quiet. Contact your avian veterinarian's office.

Bleeding

A bird can only withstand about a 20 percent loss of blood volume (in a budgie, about twelve drops) and still recover from an injury. In the event of external bleeding, you will see blood on the bird, its cage and its surroundings. In the case of internal bleeding, the bird may pass bloody droppings or bleed from its nose, mouth or vent.

For external bleeding, apply direct pressure. If the bleeding doesn't stop with direct pressure, apply a coagulant, such as styptic powder (for nails and beaks) or cornstarch (for broken feathers and skin injuries). If the bleeding stops, observe the bird to make sure the bleeding does not resume and the bird does not go into shock. Call your veterinarian's office if the bird seems weak or if it has lost a lot of blood and arrange to take the bird in for further treatment.

In the case of broken blood feathers, you may have to remove the feather shaft to stop the bleeding. To do this, grasp the feather shaft as close to the skin as you can with a pair of needle-nosed pliers and pull out the shaft with a swift, steady motion. Apply direct pressure to the skin after you remove the feather shaft.

> **First Aid Kit**
>
> I suggest that you assemble a bird owner's first aid kit so that you will have some basic supplies on hand before your bird needs them. Here's what to include:
>
> - appropriate-sized towels for catching and holding your bird
> - a heating pad, heat lamp or other heat source
> - styptic powder, silver nitrate stick or cornstarch to stop bleeding (use styptic powder and silver nitrate stick on beak and nails only)
> - blunt-tipped scissors
> - nail clippers and nail file
> - blunt-end tweezers
> - hydrogen peroxide or other disinfectant solution
> - eye irrigation solution
> - bandage materials such as gauze squares, masking tape (it doesn't stick to a bird's feathers like adhesive tape does) and gauze rolls
> - Pedialyte or other energy supplement
> - eye dropper
> - penlight

Breathing Problems

Respiratory problems in pet birds can be life threatening. The bird wheezes or clicks while breathing, bobs its tail, breathes with an open mouth, and has discharge from its nares or swelling around its eyes.

Keep the bird warm, place it in a bathroom with a hot shower running to help it breathe easier and call your veterinarian's office.

Burns

Birds that are burned severely enough can go into shock and may die. A burned bird has reddened skin and burnt or greasy feathers. The bird may also show signs of shock (see below for details).

Mist burned area with cool water. Apply antibiotic cream or spray lightly. **Do not apply any oily or greasy substances,** including butter. Contact your veterinarian's office immediately for further instructions.

Concussion

A concussion results from a sharp blow to the head that can cause injury to the brain. Birds sometimes suffer concussions when they fly into mirrors or windows. They will seem stunned and may go into shock.

Keep the bird warm, prevent it from hurting itself further and watch it carefully. Alert your veterinarian's office to the injury.

Eye Injury

Untreated eye problems may lead to blindness. Symptoms include swollen or pasty eyelids, discharge, cloudy eyeball, increased rubbing of eye area.

Examine the eye carefully for foreign bodies. Contact your veterinarian for more information.

Fractures

A fracture can cause a bird to go into shock. Depending on the type of fracture, infections can also set in. Birds most often break bones in their legs, so be on the lookout for a bird that is holding one leg at an odd angle or that isn't putting weight on one leg. Sudden swelling of a leg or wing, or a droopy wing can also indicate fractures.

Confine the bird to its cage or a small carrier. Don't handle it unnecessarily. Keep it warm and contact your veterinarian.

Lead Poisoning

Birds can die from lead poisoning, so keep your budgie away from items containing lead, such as stained glass, leaded paint and fishing and drapery weights.

Overheating

High body temperatures can kill a bird. An overheated bird will try to make itself thin. It will hold its wings away from its body, open its mouth and roll its tongue in an attempt to cool itself. Birds don't have sweat glands, so they must try to cool their bodies by exposing as much of their skin's surface as they can to moving air. Cool the bird off by putting it in front of a fan (make sure the blades are screened so the bird doesn't injure itself further), by spraying it with cool water or by having it stand in a bowl of cool water. Let the bird drink cool water if it can (if it can't, offer it cool water with an eyedropper) and contact your veterinarian.

Stained glass can be dangerous to your budgie because of the lead content.

Poisoning

Poisons can kill a small bird quickly. Poisoned birds may suddenly regurgitate, have diarrhea or bloody droppings, and have redness or burns around their mouths. They may also go into convulsions, become paralyzed or go into shock. Put the poison out of your bird's reach. Contact your veterinarian for further instructions. Be prepared to take the poison with you to the vet's office in case he or she needs to contact a poison control center.

Seizures

Seizures can indicate a number of serious conditions, including lead poisoning, infections, nutritional deficiency, heat stroke and epilepsy. The bird goes into a seizure that lasts from a few seconds to a minute. Afterward, it seems dazed and may stay on the cage floor for several hours. It may also appear unsteady and won't perch.

Keep the bird from hurting itself further by removing everything you can from its cage. Cover the bird's cage with a towel and darken the room to reduce the bird's stress level. Contact your veterinarian's office for further instructions immediately.

Shock

Shock indicates that the bird's circulatory system cannot move the blood supply around the bird's body. This is a serious condition that can lead to death if left untreated. A bird in shock may act depressed, may breathe rapidly and may have a fluffed appearance. If your bird displays these signs in conjunction with a recent accident, suspect shock and take appropriate action.

Keep your bird warm, cover its cage and transport it to your veterinarian's office as soon as possible.

Caring for Older Birds

Older pet birds are prone to a number of health problems, including tumors, vision problems, thyroid gland insufficiencies, chlamydiosis and upper respiratory infections.

Tumors

Budgies can develop tumors as early as age five, although if a bird passes the age of seven without developing a tumor, it will probably live out its life tumor free. If you notice that your pet's breastbone sticks out a little more than it used to or that your bird has difficulty perching, schedule an evaluation with your avian veterinarian; both of these signs indicate possible tumor development.

Vision Problems

Vision problems can show themselves in several ways. Your pet may no longer be able to judge distances well, or its eyes may appear clouded over. Just as in older people, cataracts can appear in older budgies.

Thyroid Problems

Thyroid problems occur in two main areas: a deficiency in the bird's hormonal system or a need for supplemental iodine in the diet. If your budgie suddenly gains weight and develops fat deposits that resemble tumors, contact your avian veterinarian to have your pet examined.

Although they may not seem to be connected, a thyroid problem may show itself in a longer-than-average molt. If you notice that your budgie's molting period seems unusually long as it ages, talk to your avian veterinarian. A hormonal supplement may help keep your bird healthy.

Although older budgies are far from being delicate "hothouse flowers," owners of these birds should pay more attention to their pets' diets to ensure that the bird continues to receive a varied diet that is low in fat. Owners should also monitor the temperature of the room in which the bird is kept during cool weather. Add supplemental heat by using an incandescent bulb covered with a reflector on one end of your bird's cage. This allows a bird to move closer to the heat source if it is cold and away from it if the bird becomes too warm. Make sure that the bulb is far enough away from the cage so that your pet cannot burn itself on the reflector or the bulb.

As your budgie ages, the need to watch its daily routine becomes even more important, since health problems that are caught early are easier to treat.

part three
Enjoying Your

Budgie

chapter 7

Budgie
Behavior

Common Budgie Behaviors

The following common budgerigar behaviors are listed in alphabetical order to help you better understand your new feathered friend!

Beak Grinding

If you hear your bird making odd little grinding noises as it's drifting off to sleep, don't be alarmed! Beak grinding is a sign of a contented budgie, and it's commonly heard as a bird settles in for the night.

Beak Wiping

After a meal, it's common for a budgie to wipe its beak against a perch or on the cage floor to clean it. If something particularly persistent is stuck to a budgie's beak, it will use its foot to clean its beak.

Birdie Aerobics

This is how I describe a sudden bout of stretching that all parrots seem prone to. An otherwise calm bird will suddenly grab the cage bars and stretch the wing and leg muscles on one side of its body, or it will raise both wings high.

Eye Pinning

This is what happens when your budgie sees something that excites it. Its pupils will be large, then contract, then go large again. Birds will pin their eyes when they see a favorite food, a favored person, another bird or a special toy. In larger parrots, this can also be a sign of confused emotions that can leave an owner vulnerable to a nasty bite. Your budgie may also bite when it's in "emotional overload," so watch out!

Feather Picking

Don't confuse this with preening (see below). Feather picking results from physiological problems, such as a dietary imbalance, a hormonal change, a thyroid problem or a infection of the skin or feathers. It can also be caused by an emotional upset, such as a change in the owner's appearance, a change in the bird's routine, another pet being added to the home, a new baby in the home or a number of other factors. Once feather picking begins, it may be difficult to get a bird to stop. Although it looks painful to us, some birds find the routine of pulling out their feathers emotionally soothing. The good news is that budgies are not as prone to this condition as larger parrots are. If you keep more than one budgie, however, be aware that they

> **Feathered Warnings**
>
> Your bird's feathers are one of the most fascinating organs of its body. The bird uses feathers for movement, warmth and balance, among other things. The following are some feather-related behaviors that can indicate health problems for your budgie.
>
> Fluffing: A healthy budgie will fluff before preening or for short periods. If your budgie seems to remain fluffed up for an extended period, see your avian veterinarian. This can be a sign of illness in birds.
>
> Mutual preening: Two birds will preen each other affectionately, but if you notice excessive feather loss, make sure one bird is not picking on the other and pulling out healthy feathers.
>
> Preening: A healthy bird will preen often to keep its feathers in top shape. However, a bird under stress may start to preen excessively and severe feather loss can result.

sometimes pick out each other's feathers. If this occurs, you may have to house your birds in separate cages to allow the plucked bird to regrow its plumage.

Fluffing

This is often a prelude to preening or a tension releaser. If your bird fluffs up, stays fluffed and resembles a little feathered pinecone, however, contact your avian veterinarian for an appointment because fluffed feathers can be an indicator of illness.

Jealousy

Some budgies become very possessive of their owners, and these jealous birds demonstrate their displeasure in a number of ways. These can include tearing up their cages, nibbling on their owners' hands or screaming that, while not as annoying as the noise made by a cockatoo or macaw, can nonetheless diminish your enjoyment of your budgie as a pet. To prevent your budgie from becoming a problem pet, be sure to provide it the opportunity to entertain itself in its cage alone from time to time. Don't reward its screaming for attention (you'll soon learn which screams are just for the joy of making noise and which ones indicate a pet in danger or pain), and don't bribe your pet into silence with treats while you are out of the room or on the phone. If you do, your bird will soon have you wrapped around its wing feathers and will take full advantage of the situation.

Mutual preening is an honor the budgie reserves only for its favorite companions. If your budgie tries to preen you, consider it a sign of great affection!

Mutual Preening

This is part of the preening behavior described below, and it can take place between birds or between birds and their owners. It is a sign of affection reserved for best friends or mates, so consider it an honor if your budgie wants to preen your eyebrows, hair, mustache or beard, or your arms and hands.

Pair Bonding

Not only mated pairs bond, but best bird buddies of the same sex will demonstrate some of the same behavior, including sitting close to each other, preening each other and mimicking the other's actions, such as stretching or scratching, often at the same time.

Your budgie preens to keep its feathers healthy and clean.

Preening

This is part of a budgie's normal routine. You will see your bird ruffling and straightening its feathers each day. It will also take oil from the uropygial or preen gland at the base of its tail and put the oil on the rest of its feathers, so don't be concerned if you see your pet seeming to peck or bite at its tail. If, during molting, your bird seems to remove whole feathers, don't panic! Old, worn feathers are pushed out by incoming new ones, which makes the old feathers loose and easy to remove.

Regurgitating

If you see that your bird is pinning its eyes, bobbing its head and pumping its neck and crop muscles, it is about to regurgitate some food for you. Birds regurgitate to their mates during breeding season and to their young while raising chicks. It is a mark of great affection to have your bird regurgitate its dinner for you, so try not to be too disgusted if your pet starts bringing up its last meal for you.

Resting On One Foot

Do not be alarmed if you see your budgie occasionally resting on only one foot. This is normal behavior (the resting foot is often drawn up into the belly feathers). If you see your bird always using both feet to perch, please contact your avian veterinarian because this can indicate a health problem.

Scratching

Budgies have remarkably flexible leg joints, which they sometimes use to bring their legs up and behind their wings to scratch their heads. Budgies may be the only psittacine birds that do this; larger parrots bring their heads and feet together in front of their bodies to scratch.

Stress

Stress can show itself in many ways in your bird's behavior, including shaking, diarrhea, rapid breathing, wing and tail fanning, screaming, feather picking, poor sleeping habits or loss of appetite. Over a period of time, stress can harm your budgie's health. To prevent your bird from becoming stressed, try to provide it with as normal and regular a routine as possible. Parrots are, for the most part, creatures of habit, and they don't always adapt well to sudden changes in their environment or schedule. But if you do have to change something, talk to your parrot about it first. I know it seems crazy, but telling your bird what you're going to do before you do it may actually help reduce its stress. I received this advice from avian behaviorist Christine Davis, and now I explain what I'm doing every time I rearrange the living room or leave my bird at the vet's office for boarding during business trips. If you're going to be away on vacation, tell your bird how long you'll be gone, and count the days out on your fingers in front of the bird or show it a calendar.

Vocalization

Many parrots vocalize around sunrise and sunset, which I believe hearkens back to flock behavior in the wild when wild parrots call to each other to start and end their days. Budgies are no exceptions to this rule, especially at day's end when they chirp softly as they ready themselves for sleep. You may also notice if you keep more than one budgie that the birds will call to each other during the day if they are in separate rooms (perhaps one is on a playgym in the family room while the other is in its cage in the dining room). These contact calls help birds keep track of each other, both in the wild and in your home. If something startles your budgie, you may hear it make a short, shrill call to signal that something has alarmed it. Budgies can also express their pleasure or displeasure through vocalization. Soft chirps indicate a happy bird, while shrieks indicate that something is amiss in your bird's world.

Your budgie's vocalizations are good indicators of its mental state.

Taming Your Budgie

Training a budgie (or any bird) takes a great deal of time and patience on the part of the bird owner. You must first gain your pet's trust, and then you must work to never lose it. To maintain this, you must be careful not to lose your temper with your bird and *never* hit it. Birds are very sensitive, intelligent creatures that do not deserve to be hit, no matter how you may feel in a moment of anger.

Although parrots are clever creatures, they are not linear "cause and effect" thinkers. If a parrot commits action A

7

Enjoying Your Budgie

(chewing on some molding under your kitchen cabinets, for example), it won't associate reaction B (you yelling at it, locking it in its cage or otherwise punishing it) with the original misbehavior. As a result, most traditional forms of discipline are ineffective with parrots.

So what do you do when your budgie misbehaves? Try to catch it in the act. Look at it sternly (what bird behaviorist Sally Blanchard calls "the evil eye") and tell it "No" in a firm voice. If the bird is climbing on or chewing something it shouldn't, also remove it from the source of danger and temptation as you tell it "No." If your bird has wound itself up into a screaming banshee, sometimes a little "time out" in its cage (between five and ten minutes in most cases) with the cover on does wonders to calm it down. Once the screaming stops and the bird calms down enough to play quietly, eat or simply move around its cage, the cover comes off to reveal a well-behaved, calmed-down pet.

A good first step in taming your budgie is getting it to become comfortable around you. To do this, give your bird a bit of warning before you approach its cage. Don't sneak up on your bird, and try not to startle it. Call its name when you walk into the room. Try to be quiet and to move slowly around your pet because these gestures will help it become more comfortable with you. Keep your hands behind you, and reassure the bird that you aren't there to harm it, that everything is all right and that it's a wonderful pet.

"Time-out" in a covered cage can help calm down excited birds.

After your bird is comfortable having you in the same room with it, you may want to try placing your hand in its cage as a first step toward taking it out of its cage. Place your hand in your bird's cage and hold it there for a few seconds. Don't be surprised if your bird flutters around and squawks at first at the "intruder."

7

Budgie Behavior

Continue this process daily, and leave your hand in the cage for slightly longer periods of time each day. Within a few days, your budgie won't make a fuss about your hand being in its space, and it may come over to investigate this new perch. Do not remove your hand from the bird cage the first time your budgie lands on it; just let the bird become accustomed to perching on your hand.

After several successful perching attempts on successive days, try to take your hand out of the cage with your bird on it. Some budgies will take to this new adventure willingly, while others are reluctant to leave the safety and security of home. (Be sure your bird's wings are clipped and all doors and windows are secured before taking your bird out of its cage.)

If your bird doesn't seem to respond to this method, you can try an alternate taming method. Take the bird out of its cage and into a small room, such as a bathroom, that has been bird-proofed (i.e., the toilet lid is down, the shower door is closed and the bathroom hasn't been cleaned with any cleansers with strong chemical odors recently). Sit down on the floor, place your bird in front of you and begin playing with the bird. Don't be surprised if your bird tries to fly a few times. With clipped wings, however, it won't get very far and will give up trying after a few failed attempts.

Calm your budgie down by holding it on your chest where it can hear your heartbeat.

Breeder Charlene Beane has demonstrated her budgie taming method for me several times, and its simplicity and effectiveness always amazes me. Charlene will hold a bird that isn't quite tame close to her chest so the bird can hear her heartbeat, which seems to calm the bird. She then talks to it in a low, soothing tone and explains to it that it will make someone a wonderful pet. As she does this, she gently begins to stroke the budgie's back, which helps the bird to relax. She

7

Enjoying Your Budgie

continues to explain its role as a perfect pet for about five minutes, stroking it as she talks. Pretty soon, the bird is calm and ready to be handled.

Once you've calmed your budgie using Charlene's methods, see if you can make perching on your hand a game for your pet. Once it masters perching on your hand, you can teach it to step up by gently press-ing your finger up and into the bird's belly. This will cause the bird to step up. As it does so, say "Step up" or "Up." Before long, your bird will respond to this command without much prompting.

Along with the "Up" command, you may want to teach your budgie the "Down" command. When you put the bird down on its cage or play-gym, simply say "Down" as the bird steps off your hand. These two simple commands offer a great deal of control for you over your bird, because you can say "Up" to put an unruly bird back in its cage or you can tell a parrot that needs to go to bed "Down" as you put the bird in its cage at night.

After your bird has mastered the "Up" and "Down" commands, encourage it to climb a "ladder" by moving it from index finger to index finger (the "rungs"). Keep taming sessions short (about ten minutes is the maximum budgie attention span) and make the taming process fun because it will be much more enjoyable for both of you.

To teach your budgie the "Up" command, hold a finger to its abdomen while it is perching on your finger.

After your pet has become comfortable sitting on your hand, try petting it. Birds seem to like to have their heads, backs, cheek patches, under wing areas and eye areas (including the closed eyelids) scratched or petted lightly. Quite a few like to have a spot low on their backs at the bases of their tails (over their preen glands) rubbed. Many birds do not enjoy having their stomachs scratched, although yours may think this is heaven! You'll have to experiment to see where your bird likes to be petted. You'll know you're successful if your bird clicks or grinds its beak, pins its eyes or settles onto your hand or into your lap with a completely relaxed, blissful expression on its face.

Toilet Training

Although some people don't believe it, budgies and other parrots can be toilet trained so they don't defecate on their owners. If you want to toilet train your bird, you will have to choose a word that will indicate the act of defecating to your pet, such as "Go poop" or "Go potty." While you're training your pet to associate the chosen phrase with the action, you will have to train yourself to your budgie's body language and actions that indicate it is about to defecate, such as shifting around or squatting slightly.

Once your bird seems to associate "Go potty" with defecating, you can try picking it up and holding it until it starts to shift or squat. Tell the bird to "Go potty" while placing it on its cage, where it can defecate. Once it's done, pick it up again and praise it for being such a smart bird! Expect a few accidents while you are both learning this trick, and soon you'll have a toilet-trained bird that you can put on its cage about every twenty minutes or so, give it the command and expect the bird to defecate on command.

Will My Budgie Talk?

One of the most appealing aspects of budgie ownership is this species' reputation as talented talkers. Although many budgies learn to talk, none of them is guaranteed to talk. The tips offered below will help you teach your budgie to talk, but please don't be disappointed if your pet never utters a word.

Remember that language, whether it's budgie or human, helps members of a species or group communicate. Most baby birds learn the language of their parents because it helps them communicate within their family and their flock. A pet budgie raised with people may learn to imitate the sounds it hears its human family make, but if you have more than one budgie, the birds may find communicating with each other easier and seemingly more enjoyable than trying to learn your language. By the same token, you may want to avoid giving your budgie mirror toys. If the budgie can see him or herself in the mirror, he or she will be more likely to bond with this "cage mate" than with you.

According to budgie breeder Penny Corbett, the best time to teach a budgie to talk is between the time it leaves the nest and its first birthday. If you have an adult budgie, the chances of it learning to talk are less than if you start with a young bird. Male birds may be more likely to talk, but I have heard of some talkative females, too.

> ### Dr. Irene Pepperberg and Alex
>
> An African grey named Alex, who is being studied by Irene M. Pepperberg, PhD, at the University of Arizona, has a 100-word vocabulary, can count to six and correctly answer questions about the size, shape, color and number of objects shown him. He can categorize objects, telling a questioner what traits the objects have in common or how they differ. Not bad for a "birdbrain"!

Start with a young bird because the younger the bird is, the more likely it is to want to mimic human speech.

Pick one phrase to start with. Keep it short and simple, such as the bird's name. Say the phrase slowly so that the bird learns it clearly. Some people teach their budgies to talk by rattling off words and phrases quickly, only to be disappointed when the bird repeats them in a blurred jumble that cannot be understood.

Be sure to say the chosen phrase with emphasis and enthusiasm. Birds like a "drama reward" and seem to learn words that are said emphatically, which may be why some of them pick up bad language so quickly!

Try to have phrases make sense. For instance, say "Good morning" or "Hello" when you uncover the bird's cage each day. Say "Good-bye" when you leave the room, or ask "Want a treat?" when you offer your budgie its meals.

Don't change the phrase around. If you're teaching your bird to say "Hello," for example, don't say "Hello" one day, then "Hi" the next, followed by "Hi Petey!" (or whatever your bird's name is) another day.

Keep training sessions short. Budgie breeders recommend ten- to fifteen-minute sessions.

Train your bird in a quiet area. Think of how distracting it is when someone is trying to talk to you with a radio or television blaring in the background. Your budgie won't be able to hear you any better or understand what you are trying to accomplish if you try to train it in the midst of noisy distractions. Be sure to keep your budgie involved in your family's routine, though, because isolating it completely won't help it feel comfortable and part of the family. Remember that a bird needs to feel comfortable in its environment before it will draw attention to itself by talking.

Be patient with your pet. Stop the sessions if you find you are getting frustrated. Your budgie will sense that something is bothering you and will react by becoming bothered itself. This is not an ideal situation for you or your bird. Try to keep your mood upbeat. Smile a lot and praise your pet when it does well!

When you aren't talking to your budgie, try listening to it. Budgies and other birds sometimes mumble to themselves to practice talking as they drift off to sleep. Because a budgie has a very small voice, you'll have to listen carefully to hear if your pet is making progress.

Finally, if your patient, consistent training seems to be going nowhere, you may have to accept the fact that your budgie isn't going to talk. We finally had to do this with my budgie, Charlie. Despite my mother's most patient attempts to teach the bird to say "Pretty bird," he never learned to talk. My mother did things by the book, too. She spoke in a bright, cheerful voice, she kept the training sessions short, she kept

If you are hoping to get your budgie to talk, avoid mirror toys. Your bird may bond with your budgie in the mirror rather than you.

7

Enjoying Your Budgie

a positive attitude and tone when talking to the bird, and she displayed patience that rivaled Job's, but Charlie remained silent. Perhaps he was too old, perhaps he was too isolated, or perhaps he just wasn't interested in the phrase.

As I've said before, don't be too disappointed if your pet doesn't learn to talk. As one *Bird Talk* reader explained it, "talking should be the icing on the cake," rather than the primary reason for own-ing a bird. If you end up with a non-talking pet, continue to love it for the unique creature that it is, rather than what you want it to be.

Talking Success Stories

Puck, a budgie in northern California, holds the Guinness World Record for largest vocabulary by an animal. Puck's owner estimates that her bird has a 1,728-word vocabulary!

Sparkie, a budgie that lived in Great Britain from 1954 to 1962, held the record for a talking bird in his time. He won the BBC's Cage Word Contest in 1958 by reciting eight four-line nursery rhymes without stopping. At the time of his death, Sparkie had a vocabulary of 531 words and 383 sentences.

part four

Beyond the Basics

chapter 8

For More Information

For more information on bird care, look for these books at your local library, bookstore or pet store:

Alderton, David, with illustrations by Graeme Stevenson. *Atlas of Parrots of the World*. 1991. TFH Publications Inc.

———*Birdkeeper's Guide to Budgies*. 1988. Tetra Press.

———*Birdkeeper's Guide to Parrots and Macaws*. 1989. Tetra Press.

———*You and Your Pet Bird*. 1994. Alfred A. Knopf.

Birmelin, Immanuel, and Annette Wolter. *The New Parakeet Handbook*. 1986. Barron's Educational Series Inc.

Gallerstein, Gary A. DVM. *The Complete Bird Owner's Handbook*. 1994. Howell Book House.

Magazines

Bird Breeder. Bimonthly magazine dedicated to the concerns of bird breeders who raise and sell pet birds. Subscription information: P.O. Box 420235, Palm Coast, FL 32142-0235.

Bird Talk. Monthly magazine devoted to pet bird ownership. Subscription information: P.O. Box 57347, Boulder, CO 80322-7347.

Birds USA. Annual magazine aimed at first-time bird owners. Look for it in your local bookstore or pet store.

Caged Bird Hobbyist. This magazine for pet bird owners is published seven times a year. Subscription information: 5400 NW 84 Ave., Miami, FL 33166-3333.

Parakeets YearBOOK. Published by yearBOOKS Inc., 1 TFH Plaza, Neptune, NJ 07753. Look for it in your local pet store or bookstore.

Online Resources

Bird-specific sites have been cropping up regularly on the Internet. These sites offer pet bird owners the opportunity to share stories about their pets, along with trading helpful hints about bird care.

If you belong to an online service, look for the pet site (it's sometimes included in more general topics, such as "Hobbies and Interests," or more specifically "Pets") If you have Internet access, use your Web browser or WebCrawler to search for "parrots" or "pet birds."

Bird Clubs

The American Budgerigar Society
1704 Kangaroo
Killeen, TX 76543

The American Federation of Aviculture
P.O. Box 56218
Phoenix, AZ 85079-6128

Australian Aviculture
52 Harris Rd.
Elliminyt, Victoria 3249, Australia

Avicultural Society of America
P.O. Box 5516
Riverside, CA 92517-5517

International Avicultural Society
P.O. Box 280383
Memphis, TN 38168

Society of Parrot Breeders and Exhibitors
P.O. Box 369
Groton, MA 01450